CHRISTIAN LIVING
Beyond Belief

Biblical Principles
for the Life of Faith

Cliff McManis

Kress Christian
PUBLICATIONS

Christian Living Beyond Belief: Biblical Principles for the Life of Faith

©2006 Cliff McManis

Published by:
Kress Christian
PUBLICATIONS
P.O. Box 132228
The Woodlands, TX 77393
www.KressChristianPublications.com

ISBN 0-9772262-2-0

Cover Design: Jerome Kayl and The Layne Moore Group
Text Design: The Layne Moore Group

This work is dedicated to
John MacArthur, Jr.,
faithful pastor, teacher and mentor

Acknowledgments

I want to thank Dan Seitz for encouraging me to pursue this project and for writing chapter 8—"Study!"

Thanks to Nancy Simpson and Dick Smith, who both have the gift of suggestions and employed them diligently in the editorial process. Also, thanks to the History of Israel class in the corporate effort of proofreading. Others made valuable suggestions that improved the manuscript: Bruce Blakey, Bob Douglas, Ray Garland, Kay Tokar and Gary Beals.

Thanks to Jim George for pointing me to Rick Kress.

And thanks to Rick Kress, of Kress Christian Publishing, for taking a step of faith to produce this work as a means of getting the truths of the Word of God in the hands of His people, for His glory (1 Corinthians 10:31).

Most of all, thanks to Debbie – my "excellent wife," soul-mate, ministry partner and best friend.

Preface

When a person accepts Jesus Christ as their personal Savior, there is usually an initial period where that person feels a sense of release and the presence of the Holy Spirit in a way never known before. But it also ushers in a number of questions: Can I possibly lose my salvation? What is prayer and what does it mean to me? If the Bible is God's Word, how can I understand what it is saying? Why is membership in a local church important? How can I grow in my Christian walk? What should my relationship be with other Christians?

Pastor Cliff McManis has tackled the formidable task of addressing and answering these and similar questions in *Christian Living Beyond Belief*. The reader will be delighted to discover that this work is a virtual primer on living the Christian life. Cliff has been a teaching pastor and Pastor of Family Ministries at the First Baptist Church of Los Altos, located in the San Francisco Bay area of Northern California for the past five years. His elective Bible classes for adults desiring a deeper understanding of Christian doctrine have always had a large and enthusiastic following because church members appreciated his thorough research, sound teaching and breadth of knowledge about other religions and how they related to our Christian faith.

Christian Living Beyond Belief will be of inestimable value to individuals just beginning their walk of faith. It is the kind of book one can pick up at any time and quickly access an area of interest or concern and find a solid Biblical basis for how that particular issue should be addressed. Virtually every statement is backed up with multiple Scripture references and real life examples from Cliff's experiences as a pastor.

However, this book is by no means limited to new Christians. Christian leaders, particularly anyone involved in Christian counseling, will find *Christian Living Beyond Belief* an invaluable resource. The book itself is a highly practical and workable tool that can be utilized by both the counselor and counselee in order to research or work through a particular question or issue. Again, the main benefit of this work is the strong scriptural documentation it affords along with practical applications.

Christian Living Beyond Belief is a gem to enjoy slowly, over time for most people. For those new to the faith, it is something to go to when you are not sure just where to turn. Here, you will find most of the answers to questions about how to live the Christian life victoriously. For the Christian leader or counselor, it is a comforting resource to have on hand, one that will help organize and distill biblical wisdom for all those who seek it.

Ray Garland
Board Chairman
First Baptist Church of Los Altos
November, 2005

Introduction

Why This Book Was Written

Since the early 1980's the Evangelical church has been infatuated with the concept of "church growth." Three decades later many Christians and church leaders still seem to have an insatiable love affair with the idea evidenced by the incessant barrage of books, seminars, conferences and propaganda on the topic. The dinning refrain of "Bigger is better!" has become the apparent battle-cry, mantra, and even the goal of countless Christian churches. Large crowds, mammoth facilities, bulging memberships, and high-profile, popular pastors are said to be evidences of true spiritual blessing in the church.

The emphasis in this whole perspective is on numerical growth and the breadth of expansion. It's focused on outward, superficial increases—that may or may not be genuine or lasting.

Such was not the mindset of Jesus, the Apostles, the early church or the New Testament. Regarding those who would believe in Christ and follow Him, Jesus said categorically, "small is the gate and narrow the road that leads to life, and only a few find it" (Matthew 7:14). By that statement Jesus was warning His disciples that the Christian message would not be popular or well received by humanity at large. Only a few people—a small number in comparison to those who hear—will actually accept it, believe and follow Christ. As a matter of fact, Jesus even got more gloomy and pessimistic with His disciples just before His death when He told them "the world hates you" (John 15:19). That comment is not in the modern day "church growth" lexicon or playbook, nonetheless, it is true. Jesus knew what He was talking about. He knows everything—He is God and the Lord of the church (Acts 20:28).

But Jesus was not anti church growth altogether. The church is a "body" (Ephesians 4:12)—a living entity. And that which is alive must grow to thrive and perpetuate. Jesus expected the church to grow.

In Matthew 16:18 Jesus promised that He would build His church and that nothing—not even hell—would prevail against it. He has kept His promise. The church has survived the onslaught of evil for 2,000 years. And the church will continue to grow, mature and prevail until Christ returns, at which time He will perfect His precious Bride.

As Jesus builds His church, every Christian has the privilege of being a part of the process. For Christ builds His church—or "Body"—with one individual believer at a time. Every Christian is an indispensable heavenly brick in the eternal Temple of God. This is exactly what Peter meant when he said, "you also, like living stones, are being built into a spiritual house to be a holy priesthood, offering spiritual sacrifices acceptable to God through Jesus Christ" (1 Peter 2:5).

Here is a basic, yet huge principle of true biblical church growth that is frequently overlooked: corporate church growth is contingent upon and augmented by individual and personal growth. For the body at large to grow, first the individual members need to grow. Tiny cells are the building blocks that enable the whole human body to grow as a unit. So it is in the church. If we want strong, growing churches then the emphasis needs to be on cultivating and encouraging spiritually healthy, mature individual Christians. We need to focus on depth, not breadth. We need to go deeper before we go wider. Many churches have it backwards. They believe individual growth flows from corporate growth, when just the opposite is true—corporate growth is a natural spiritual byproduct of personal Christian growth.

That's what this book is about. It is a study of the basic principles for individual growth in the Christian life. But individual spiritual growth does not happen in a vacuum or independent of the whole community of believers. Individual spiritual growth flourishes and reaches its zenith when the spiritual disciplines are practiced in the context of the local church, for the church is the direct conduit to God's enabling power on earth (1 Timothy 3:15). So this book also emphasizes the importance of every Christian's responsibility to grow in tandem with the local church. God intended all of us to grow together—interdependently—just like the cells of a body. A Christian who is not affiliated in a dynamic, intimate, ongoing manner with a local church is a living contradiction and is not growing to the potential God intends.

God expects, and even empowers, every Christian to progressively mature and grow in the faith during this life. This is clear from Philippians which commands every Christian "to work out your salvation with fear and trembling" (2:12). In this statement Paul meant that every Christian is obligated to engage in the process of growing as a Christian. Every believer is expected to learn the priorities of living out the Christian life in a way that honors God and glorifies Christ. God has clearly shown in

His Word, the Bible, what the basics are for each Christian to grow spiritually.

Individual Christian growth comes through the life-long, consistent practice of the spiritual disciplines. The spiritual disciplines are simply prioritized virtues for daily living. These virtues are clearly taught in the Bible, were modeled perfectly by Christ, were preached by the first Apostles, and were implemented in the early church. And it is through these disciplines that Jesus will continue to build His church, one believer at a time.

If your desire is to grow as a believer, mature in the faith, please Christ, have the fullness of the Christian life and walk confidently in the will of God, then this study is for you. There are many books on Christian growth. Some are great and some are not so great. To add to that growing canon of literature, I offer this book as a fresh study to aid you in the process.

How to Use This Book

This book is designed to be a tool. It's chapters are the byproduct of more than fifteen years of bible teaching, counseling and ministry. As I continue to shepherd God's people, I am always looking for practical tools to facilitate ministry on behalf of the saints.

One area I repeatedly find myself emphasizing with Christians as I counsel them is in the area of personal spiritual development. It seems that more and more believers I counsel do not have any formal approach to practicing the basic biblical virtues for growth. Many have no regular, daily prayer life. Many more neglect regular, daily Bible reading of any substance. They are not talking to God, and they are not listening to God. No wonder they aren't growing! No wonder they are miserable, lacking fulfillment and not experiencing victory in their spiritual development. You cannot successfully live the Christian life apart from how God said you should live it.

This book is a blueprint and roadmap for spiritual growth that God has outlined in His Word. I have distilled the basics of Christian living into eleven chapters and have practical application questions at the end of each chapter. The questions are designed to force the reader to interact with God's truth by applying it to daily living. The questions can be a dynamic catalyst for growth if the answers are written out in complete sentences and then discussed. So take the time to answer the questions.

Write in the book. Writing out thoughts clarifies thinking, makes application of truth concrete, and makes the reader accountable. Writing yields an inescapable permanence to what we think about something. It forces one to think at a deeper level—and as a result God can bring greater conviction and deeper spiritual transformation.

It would also be ideal to read this book with someone else. Hold each other accountable. Read a chapter a week. Use it to spur one another on to love and good deeds (Hebrews 10:24). Use it as a mentoring or discipling tool. Use this book for your small accountability group. Use it as a text for your Sunday school class. Use the questions to lead discussion groups in home Bible studies. The options are endless.

Also, when you read this book have your Bible open. Examine everything to see if it matches up to God's Word. Bible references are given on every page for the points I wanted to make. Don't just skip over the references. Stop, open the Bible, read the verse so that God can speak to your heart. That is how God talks to us today...through His Word.

How This Book was Written
Simplicity

One of the goals I had in writing this book was to distill all the basics of Christian living down into simple, easy to understand priorities and principles. I wanted the information to be accessible to all Christians who might read this book, no matter how young or old they are in the faith; no matter how much prior biblical knowledge they may or may not have.

The Bible is profound, supernatural and complex. But at the same time, God also wanted the Bible to be understood by all His followers. Jesus spoke in the language of the common people of His day. He did not speak, preach or teach in highfalutin, incomprehensible, erudite terms that only   theological scholars could comprehend. His blessed truths were intended to be understood by even a child who has the ears and eyes of faith.

My hope is that I have been able to capture the basic biblical truths in simple ways, while retaining the Bible's life-changing power along with its profound and matchless stature.

Readability

There's nothing more frustrating than trying to go through a book that's difficult to read, for whatever reason. Maybe the book was not written well. Maybe it's too complicated. Maybe the author is over your head. Whatever the case may be, I wanted this book to be reader-friendly.

To that end I have purposefully limited all quotes to nothing but the Bible. I do not quote from third-party sources, the Church Fathers, the great reformers, the church confessions or catechisms, or even from popular Christian writers and authors of today. I limit my quotes to the Bible.

The Bible used throughout this book is the *New International Version*. Occasionally I will quote from a different translation and in such cases will indicate so in parentheses.

At other times I give my own literal translation based on the Greek of the New Testament or the Hebrew of the Old Testament. In such cases, it is my desire to illustrate clearly to the reader the beauty and relevance of the original language relative to certain passages. It is inevitable that at times the picturesque nature of a given word defies translation, or at best its original precision gets shrouded, and sometimes even lost in translation to another language.

Practicality

God wants us to read and study the Bible so that we can apply its truths to our lives and so that we might grow and change. Reading the Bible without the goal of life-change and personal application is intellectual pride and hypocrisy. Biblical truth is to be lived out in daily practice. Being a Christian has to do with living a lifestyle. With that in mind, this book was written to aid the reader in living out the Christian life, not just providing mere theoretical information. My prayer is that God, through His Holy Spirit, can make that a reality for you.

Each chapter concludes with recommendations for further study on the various topics throughout the book. Ephesians 4:11-12 says that God gave certain "gifts" to the church to help Christians grow. He specifically says that some of these gifts are "teachers." He meant spiritual teachers—men and women of God who have a unique ability of expounding and explaining biblical truth in meaningful and practical ways. The recommended resources in this book are by spiritual teachers who have proven themselves trustworthy and have exemplified doctrinal and personal integrity in the Christian life. My desire is that their writings would be a blessing to you as they have been for me.

Contents

Contents

1

Worship!

*"God is spirit, and his worshippers must
worship in spirit and in truth"*
(John 4:24)

This chapter is not about music. That may surprise many. Unfortunately today, many Christians equate "worship" with music, or vice versa. They say that the time when we sing in the Sunday service, or Sunday school is the "worship" portion. They say that church staff people who are in charge of the music and singing are the "worship" ministers. But that is a very myopic view of biblical worship. True worship incorporates more than singing. As a matter of fact, biblically, music is a secondary component of true worship. Deep, meaningful, godly worship happens all the time, or it should, without any music or singing at all.

So then, what is worship? The Bible is the authority on the subject. There is individual worship and corporate worship, both of which complement one another and are inextricably related.

The Bible teaches that all people worship. Everyone was created to worship. The question is what are you worshipping and how do you do it? God gave the Bible to humanity to answer these questions. The Creator wants His creatures to worship only Him, and to worship Him the right way. Consider the following biblical principles of true worship.

What is Worship?
True worship is defined clearly and comprehensively throughout the sixty-six books of the Bible. There are literally dozens of different

Hebrew and Greek words used in the Bible to describe the act of worship. This fact alone illustrates that true worship of God is not superficial, mechanical or one-dimensional. True worship of the living God is dynamic, variegated, vibrant and defies humanly descriptive boundaries. The act of worshipping God is like the multi-faceted diamond that reflects various rays of matchless beauty with every slight turn of the stone.

With that said, it is still possible to define biblical worship by examining a few of the most prominent words used to describe worship in the Bible. The following four words are instructive:

"Praise"- this word comes from the Greek word *aineo* and refers to giving verbal, joyful praise to God. This word is used numerous times in the Greek Old Testament (the *LXX*, also called the Septuagint) and about ten times in the New Testament. God receives verbal praise from humans (Luke 19:37), angels (Luke 2:13), individually (Luke 2:20) and corporately (Revelation 19:5). 'Praise' was a staple of early church worship, for Acts 2 states the first Christians made a priority of biblical teaching, fellowship, communion, prayer and "*praising* God" (Acts 2:42, 47).

"Glorify"- this is the Greek word *doxa* from which we get "doxology"— a hymn of praise to God. Different forms of this word are used over 160 times in the New Testament. The original Old Testament usage had to do with that which was "weighty" or which made an imprint and impression on something else. When used in reference to God, it connotes the idea that God is "weighty"—He is the Great Archetype of humanity. "Glory" speaks of God's splendor, radiance, and matchless majesty. When we "glorify" God, we are acknowledging that He is transcendent, other-worldly, supernatural, heavenly and thus worthy to receive worship from His creatures. Paul calls on all believers to "*glorify* the God and Father of our Lord Jesus Christ" with "one heart and mouth" (Romans 15:6; cf. Luke 2:20; 5:25; 18:43; Revelation 15:4; 1 Corinthians 6:20).

"Serve"- this is the Greek word *latreuo* and its noun form is *latria*. The noun is where we get the suffix *-latry*, as in 'idol + latry', which is the illegitimate worship of idols. This word is used about ninety times in the Old Testament (*LXX*) in reference to corporate and individual worship to God through acts of service flowing from a pure heart (i.e., Deuteronomy 10:12). The verb is used twenty-one times in the New Testament and always in a religious sense. It speaks of a person's spiritual service rendered to God as opposed to service rendered to man. Usually translated as "serve" or "service", occasionally it is translated as "worship." Paul testified before Governor Felix by saying, "I admit that I *worship* the God of our fathers" (Acts 24:14; cf. Philippians 3:3). The distinctive nuance of this word is its reference to spiritual ministry—good works—that we do for God resulting from a heart of gratitude for what He has done for us. Further examples are in Luke 1:74; 2:37; 4:8; Acts 27:23; Romans 1:9; 12:1; Hebrews 8:5; Revelation 7:15.

"Worship"- this is the Greek word *proskuneo* and it means "to bow down," "to fall down," "to bow toward" or "to kiss the ground." It's the most picturesque of all the words used in the Bible to describe worship. The verb is used fifty-nine times in the New Testament and always exclusively in reference to God (Revelation 5:14) or Jesus (Matthew 2:11; 14:33; 28:9). It refers to an attitude of devotion, homage and adoration made manifest through concrete, tangible acts of devotion—like bowing and kneeling. It is a way of acknowledging God and Jesus as sovereign King and Lord.

There are common themes of usage in the above four words that help define true worship. First of all, worship has to do with what we give to God—all worship is a deliberate act of giving something to God, be it verbal praise, a song of glory, spiritual acts of service, or humble adoration and devotion. Second, true worship issues from the right heart attitude. We render praise, glory, service and devotion to God out of gratitude and thanksgiving for what God has done on our behalf. So worship is a response in light of God's goodness to us. Third, true worship is directed toward God. Praise, giving glory, spiritual service, and homage are religious acts reserved for God alone who is the Creator, Savior and Judge of all men. And finally, worship is all-encompassing. It includes our words, works, motives and actions. We are to worship God with our whole life and being.

Who Should We Worship?
Worship the Father
The Bible teaches monotheism—the worship of one God. To worship anything or anyone else other than the one, true God is idolatry,

sinful and wrong. The first of the Ten Commandments makes this clear: "I am the LORD your God...You shall have no other gods before Me" (Exodus 20:2-3). God later commanded Moses, "Do not worship any other god, for the LORD, whose name is Jealous, is a jealous God" (Exodus 34:14). In this verse God uses His personal name, YHWH (also spelled 'Yahweh' or 'Jehovah'), which our English Bible translates as 'LORD' in all capital   letters. So only YHWH should be worshipped.

God tells Isaiah that He is a jealous God, just as He told Moses: "I am the LORD; that is my name! I will not give my glory to another" (42:8). God will not share the heavenly stage with anyone else. All our worship in the form of praise, devotion, veneration ('veneration' means 'worship'—don't let anyone tell you otherwise), service, requests, prayers, thanksgiving, and honor is to be directed to God alone and no one or anything else. To do so is to sin against God.

In the New Testament, Jesus revealed more information about who YHWH of the Old Testament was. The greatest revelation Jesus gave was when He spoke of God as "the Father" (John 17:5). And Jesus commanded believers to address God in prayer and worship as "Father in heaven" (Matthew 6:9). That's why Christians, since the time of the Apostles, have always prayed to God the Father (Romans 8:15; Ephesians 3:14; 1 Peter 1:3).

Worship Jesus

The Bible commands all people to worship Jesus. Psalm 2:12 says, "Kiss the Son, lest he be angry and you be destroyed in your way." The wise men, who traveled hundreds of miles from the East at the time of Christ's birth, came to honor Jesus as the Divine King. They presented gifts of royalty to Him as "they bowed down and worshipped him" (Matthew 2:11). After Jesus rose from the dead, His eleven disciples "worshipped him" on the mountain (Matthew 28:17). In the future, all creation will bow the knee to Jesus, acknowledging that He is Lord (Philippians 2:10-11). The myriad angels in heaven worship Jesus with the same reverence that is directed toward the Father (Revelation 5:11-14).

Jesus is worthy of worship because He is God—He is equal in glory and deity to the Father (John 17:5). One of the greatest revelations that came to light through Jesus' teaching is when He declared to all that He was equal with God the Father (John 10:30)—that He Himself was the YHWH of the Old Testament.

In John 8:58, Jesus proclaimed to the Jews of His day that He was the great "I AM" of the Old Testament: "I tell you the truth, before Abraham was born, I am." Jesus used two different verbs here to contrast His own divine nature with the finite, human, created nature of Abraham who lived 2,000 BC. A literal translation of this verse can be rendered as follows: "Before Abraham was created and came into existence, I AM."

When Jesus called Himself "I AM," He was referring to the name God called Himself in front of the burning bush in the days of Moses (God is referred to as "I AM" more than 6,000 times in the Old Testament!). At that time God told Moses to lead the Israelites out of Egyptian slavery.

Moses asked God, "Who shall I tell them sent me? What shall I tell them God's name is?" God answered Moses and said, "Tell them 'I AM' has sent you" (Exodus 3:14).

God told Moses that His personal name was "I AM." In the Gospel of John, Jesus refers to Himself as "I AM" more than seven times. Jesus was telling the Jews of His day that He was the God of the Old Testament, who had become incarnated as the God-Man. This is the great mystery of the ages (1 Timothy 3:16).

One of the most basic marks of false religion is the rejection of Jesus' deity. Unbiblical religions and philosophies everywhere deny that Jesus is the Almighty, eternal, Creator God who is equal to the Father. False religion refuses to give Jesus His proper place. Muslims say they believe in Jesus, but they say He was only a prophet and not God. To worship Jesus is one of the worst sins that can be committed in Islam. Mormons say they believe in Jesus, but they do not worship Jesus. They teach, rather, that they worship only the Father *through* Jesus, the Son. Mormons teach Jesus is a created being. The Jehovah's Witnesses say it is wrong, even blasphemy, to worship Jesus. They teach that Jesus is not God, but a created being.

Where all these religions go wrong is in their misunderstanding of the triune nature of God as taught in the Bible. Christianity teaches that there is one God (Deuteronomy 6:4; Exodus 20:1-3), and only He is to be worshipped. In the Old Testament God is called *Elohim* and *YHWH*. The New Testament gives further specific revelation about God's nature. It teaches that the One true God exists as three distinct, equal personalities—Father, Son and Holy Spirit (Matthew 28:19). One God, three Persons. Not three gods. Three gods would be polytheism. One God, three Divine Persons.

The one God has a plural nature—three persons. The Old Testament word *Elohim* (translated as 'God' in our English Bibles) hinted at this reality, for it's a plural Hebrew word. The *-im* ending makes it plural.

This is a mystery—impossible to fathom in the finite, fallen human mind. But it is who God said He is. It should not surprise us that the very nature of God is a mystery that defies human comprehension. For in Isaiah 9:6, God is described as "Wonderful." That is a Hebrew word that literally means "Incomprehensible." That's who God is—Incomprehensible. God told Isaiah the same thing when He said, "'For my thoughts are not your thoughts, neither are your ways my ways,' declares the LORD. 'As the heavens are higher than the earth, so are my ways higher than your ways and my thoughts than your thoughts'" (55:8-9).

So a true believer is supposed to give the same honor, worship, praise, glory, reverence and veneration to Jesus, the God-Man, that is reserved for God the Father. Doing so honors the Father (John 5:22-23).

Worship in the Spirit

The Holy Spirit plays a unique and central role in Christian worship. The Bible teaches that the Holy Spirit is God (2 Corinthians 3:17); He is to be revered (Acts 5:1-10); He is a divine Person (John 14:16-18, 26); He literally indwells every believer from the moment of conversion (Ephesians 1:13); and He co-authored the Scriptures (2 Peter 1:2-21). He is distinct from Jesus and the Father, yet equal to them in every way as Deity (Psalm 139:7-18; Job 33:4). There is no other religion on earth that believes these things about the Holy Spirit.

In the Old Testament, God literally dwelt among His people in various and sporadic ways. At times God would appear to a few select saints on an occasional basis through the Angel of the LORD (Exodus 23:20-23). At other times He would appear in a vision or dream (Genesis 15:1; 1 Samuel 3:1-15). He also appeared in a burning bush (Exodus 3:1-2), a pillar of cloud by night and a pillar of fire by day (Exodus 13:21; 34:5). At other times His Spirit would come upon prophets, priests and kings in a temporary manner to facilitate a special ministry among the people (1 Samuel 10:9-10; 16:13-14). One of the most common ways God would manifest His presence to His people in a direct way was through the "glory of the LORD." The "glory of the LORD" in the Old Testament speaks of the visible manifestation of the invisible God (Exodus 33:12-23).

In the Old Testament, the focal point of worship for God's people flowed from and around the "glory of the LORD." From the time of Moses (around 1400 B.C.), God chose to dwell among His people through the "glory of the LORD." The designated place He chose to rest was with the Ark of the Covenant (Numbers 10:33-36). The Ark was a portable chest made of acacia wood and coated with gold all around (Exodus 25:11). It was four feet long, two and a half feet wide and two and a half feet high with rings on the top four corners by which the priests could transport it with poles (Exodus 37:5). It had a lid, called "the mercy seat" (Exodus 25:17-22), made of gold with two cherub (angels) figurines on top. In the Ark were kept the two stone tablets with the Ten Commandments (Exodus 16:33; 1 Kings 8:9).

The most significant thing about the Ark was that God lived there! The LORD (or, 'YHWH') told Moses that from the mercy seat, "I will meet with you and give you all my commands" (Exodus 25:22). I Samuel 4:4 makes the amazing statement that "the LORD Almighty...is enthroned between the cherubim" on the mercy seat of the Ark of the Covenant. How could the infinite Creator of the universe live on top of a 4' x 30" x 30" box? The answer is that God chose to manifest His real presence there through "the glory of the LORD." Because this was true, Scripture says that wherever the Ark was, the very presence of God stood in the midst of the people. As such, those who did not treat it as holy were judged and even killed directly by God (1 Samuel 6:19; 2 Samuel 6:3-8).

When the Israelites were not on the move, the Ark was supposed to reside in the inner room of the Tabernacle. The Tabernacle was a big tent designed by God to serve as the focal point of all true worship. "Tabernacle" means "dwelling place" and so at the Tabernacle God would dwell among His people (Exodus 25:8-9). When Moses had finished constructing the Tabernacle according to God's blueprints, the Bible says God came down, took up residence in the tent and "the glory of the LORD filled the tabernacle" (Exodus 40:34). God literally lived there through the presence of His "glory."

About 400 years after Moses in 960 B.C., King Solomon built a Temple as God commanded (1 Kings 5:5). At that time the Ark of the Covenant was placed in a permanent building in Jerusalem after being transported in a transitory tent, over centuries, from city to city. After Solomon built the temple and dedicated it, God appeared to him and promised: "I have   consecrated this temple....My eyes and my heart will always be there" (1 Kings 9:3). God literally took up residence in the Temple through His "glory." As such, the Temple was the focal point for worship and devotion for the Israelites. It was a place of sacrifices for sin, prayer, singing and national annual feasts. The Temple was where believers went to be in the immediate presence of God.

The "glory of the LORD" continued to live in the Temple until the days of Ezekiel in the sixth century B.C. But because of repeated sin, and unspeakable acts of abomination done in God's Temple, the "glory" left the Temple permanently as an act of judgment against disobedient Israel (Ezekiel 9-11). That was the bad news. The good news is that God promised to return His glory to His people through His Holy Spirit in the days of the New Covenant. God promised that at some future time He would send His Spirit, not to live in a tent or a building, but this time inside the human heart! Of this new day, God declared: "I will give you a new heart and put a new spirit in you...and I will put my Spirit in you and move you to follow my decrees" (Ezekiel 36:26-27). Jeremiah called this promise of the indwelling Holy Spirit the "New Covenant" (31:31).

The New Covenant was instituted during the ministry of Jesus beginning with His death and resurrection (Luke 22:20). Before Jesus died and rose again, the Holy Spirit never permanently dwelled inside believers (John 7:37-39). Only after Jesus ascended into heaven and was glorified was the Holy Spirit poured out on all believers to live in them permanently (Acts 1:7-8; 2:1 ff.). Today, whenever a person believes in the gospel and trusts in Christ, the moment they believe God takes up residence, or "tabernacles," inside of them the way He took up residence in the Tabernacle and Temple building of the Old Testament. The difference now is that He will never leave the Christian once He begins living in them (Hebrews 13:5). And this is why the New Testament calls a Christian's body "the temple of the Holy Spirit" (1 Corinthians 6:19). We literally take God with us wherever we go as

Christians—so everything we do has the potential of being an act of worship before God (Romans 12:1-2).

Because every believer has the Holy Spirit of God living in them, they are able to truly worship God. They have been born again by the Holy Spirit (John 3:3-8). The indwelling Holy Spirit enables us to pray directly to God the Father, helps us understand Scripture, and He spiritually transforms us from the inside out (2 Corinthians 3:17-18). People who do not have the Holy Spirit living in them can only practice external religion. They try to conform their outward behavior in their own strength, which is not true worship. Jesus said true worship was typified by worshipping "the Father in spirit and truth...God is spirit, and his worshippers must worship in spirit and truth" (John 4:23-24). Similarly Paul said that true Christians were those "who worship by the Spirit of God, who glory in Christ Jesus, and who put no confidence in the flesh" (Philippians 3:3). You cannot truly worship God unless you have the Holy Spirit living inside of you. That's what it means to worship God in the Spirit.

Don't worship idols or icons

Recently I read one of the main news headlines about a so-called apparition of Mary, the mother of Jesus, that had appeared on the concrete wall of a Chicago highway underpass. Apparently water had been dripping down the wall for a period of time, forming a deposit made of sodium, rust and other particles. The formation, several feet long, purportedly resembles a female face, whose observers claim to be Virgin Mary. Hundreds, even thousands of people have been flocking to the newly designated alchemic shrine to offer burning candles and prayers of adoration, veneration and worship.

Such misguided religious devotion is all too common. Common sense would seem to ask, "Who would worship a dirty concrete wall of a city highway underpass here in America?" But frequently, common sense is held hostage to reality. This just goes to show that humans have a natural propensity toward false worship, and specifically toward idolatry. This is what Paul says in Romans. He shows that human rebellion is manifest most fundamentally and universally through the act of false worship. Sinners everywhere worship and serve "created things rather than the Creator" (1:25). Idolatry is rampant. It always has been.

God condemned idolatry in all of its forms in the Ten Commandments. He said,

> *You shall not make for yourself an idol in the form of anything in heaven above or on the earth beneath or in the waters below. You shall not bow down to them or worship them; for I, the LORD your God, am a jealous God, punishing the children for the sin of the fathers to the third and fourth generation of those who hate me, but showing love to a thousand [generations] of those who love me and keep my commandments (Exodus 20:4-6).*

This command specifically forbids prayer, veneration, devotion, or worship of any kind to any saintly statue, heavenly image, religious relic, or man-made cherished icon. The terminology couldn't be any more categorical. Idol worship is forbidden because God is a jealous God, and He will not share His glory with any human fabrication in the form of an idol (Nahum 1:2, 14; Deuteronomy 32:16-42). The New Testament reiterates this truth, warning Christians to keep away from religious idols (1 John 5:21).

God the Father does not have a body—He has no confined limits (John 4:24). He cannot be contained in, relegated to, or compartmentalized by any human imagery or amulets (Acts 17:24-25). He's not some impotent genie who can be confined in a bottle. He defies all human limitations and boundaries, for He is infinite (Psalm 139:1-10). Therefore, don't dishonor and belittle Him by praying to dead, man-made idols, images or icons.

Don't worship people

Scripture also condemns the worship, devotion, or veneration of any human, be they dead or alive. Praying to or communicating with dead people is called necromancy and is a form of divination. It's expressly forbidden by God and it is also dangerous. Deuteronomy warns, "Let no one be found among you who...consults the dead" (18:10-11). Consulting—by prayer, through a medium, whatever— with those who have died, in any manner is called "detestable" by God (18:12).

Despite this clear biblical injunction, some, who call themselves

"Christians," promote the practice of praying to dead believers (called 'saints') for help and guidance. Millions of people pray to Mary, who is dead, asking her for help, strength, forgiveness and even salvation. This is wrong and the practice was actually adopted right out of paganism. It has no place in Christian living. There is no example of this practice ever being performed by believers in the Bible. It is totally foreign to Scripture.

Furthermore, the Bible teaches that every true living Christian is a "saint" (Philippians 1:1). The word "saint" literally means "holy one." God makes all Christians positionally holy the moment they put their faith in Jesus Christ and become born-again (1 Corinthians 6:11; Colossians 3:12). You don't have to wait until you are dead and canonized to become a saint. If you are a Christian, then you already are a saint!

Scripture also forbids Christians to revere any living human. In the days of the early church, there was a God-fearing man named Cornelius—a centurion. One day an angel of God appeared to him and instructed him to meet the Apostle Peter. Upon meeting the great Apostle for the first time, the Bible says Cornelius "fell at [Peter's] feet in reverence" (Acts 10:25).

Peter was not flattered by this act of devotion, but rather he was agitated and made Cornelius get up off the ground: " 'Stand up,' he said, 'I am only a man myself' " (Acts 10:26). Peter knew that only God was worthy of such reverence and devotion. Keep in mind, this is Peter—the man millions of people today say was the first Pope. If any human had the right to receive and acknowledge the devotion from another person, it would have been Peter. But he rightfully condemned the notion.

Paul knew the same truth—no living human was worthy of another human's religious devotion. On one of his missionary journeys, a crowd responded positively to Paul's preaching. But they responded in the wrong manner. Instead of giving glory to the one true God, they began to venerate Paul and his associate Barnabas. When they did, Paul was grieved, tore his clothes, rushed into the crowd and rebuked their misguided reverence, saying: "Men, why are you doing this? We too are only men, human like you...turn...to the living God, who made heaven and earth" (Acts 14:14-15). Paul knew that revering humans was wrong.

Jesus taught clearly on this issue. He declared that all humans were sinful, evil, and in need of a Savior (Matthew 7:11). Every person was on a level playing field before God...all were desperately helpless in and of themselves (John 8:21-23; Matthew 19:17; cf. Romans 3:23). Therefore no individual was worthy of any special recognition or treatment, spiritually or religiously speaking. According to Jesus, all sinners were equal.

Jesus also taught that all believers were equal. He said there is only one Father—God—and all who are spiritually adopted into His family "are all brothers" (Matthew 23:8). All Christians are equal in status before Christ. There is no partiality with God (James 2:1-9; 1 Peter 1:17).

For that reason Jesus said, "do not call anyone on earth 'father,' for you have one Father, and he is in heaven" (Matthew 23:9). Despite Jesus' stern warning, millions of people today call certain religious clerics 'father.' Some religious elite, who are considered to be 'priests,' are designated with other equally exalted elitist religious titles like, 'His Holiness,' 'Holy Father' or 'Most Holy One.' These are terms that should be reserved only for God, not mere sinful, finite humans (James 3:2; Luke 5:8).

Believers need to realize that every Christian is a priest! That's what the New Testament teaches. The Apostle John wrote, "To him who loves us and has freed us from our sins by his blood and has made us to be ...*priests* to serve his God and Father" (Revelation 1:5-6). This verse is teaching that the moment a person puts trust in Jesus Christ as Savior and Lord, believing that He died on the cross in his or her place and that He rose from the dead, then immediately that person is born-again—adopted into the family of God, and is made a "priest." This promise is for every Christian, regardless of one's age, gender or marital status—the believing five year-old girl, the forty-two year-old Christian husband, as well as the God-fearing thirty year-old housewife and mother of three.

A priest is one who has immediate access to God, having the authority to go directly to Him in prayer (Hebrews 4:14-16). That privilege belongs to every Christian by virtue of faith in Christ—the Great High Priest—and because of the indwelling Holy Spirit, who resides in every Christian (1 Corinthians 6:19; Romans 8:9-10, 26-27).

So if you are a Christian, then remember that you are a sinner saved by grace who is now a saint and a priest, set apart to live a life pleasing to God. And all devotion, honor and reverence should be directed toward God and Christ alone, not toward any fellow humans—regardless of their supposed elevated spiritual stature. They have feet of clay just like you and I.

Worship with a Local Body

The Bible commands every Christian to make a priority of worshipping regularly in a local church. Hebrews 10:22 exhorts believers to "draw near to God" for corporate worship with other saints. The writer goes on to shame those Christians who have gotten into the habit of ditching church: "Let us not give up meeting together, as some are in the habit of doing, but let us encourage one another—and all the more as you see the Day approaching" (10:25). This is a command. If you are a Christian, you need to attend a local fellowship regularly.

Unfortunately the reality is that many Christians have a hit-and-miss track record when it comes to weekly church attendance. Having pastored in a few churches of various sizes and kinds, I have seen some common reasons why Christians routinely skip church. Consider some of the following:

It's not all about me

Some Christians forget the main reason for going to church. According to the Bible, the main reason to attend the corporate fellowship of believers weekly is to worship God. Church is not about what I get out of it, but it's about what I can give to God. And what God deserves, and desires, is regular, collective worship from those that He has saved.

This is what Jesus said corporate worship was all about. He declared, "a time is coming and has now come when the true worshippers will worship the Father in spirit and truth, for they are the kind of worshippers the Father seeks" (John 4:23).

God is seeking true worshippers—not false, superficial, self-centered ones. God wants believers to regularly assemble together to give Him corporate praise. This is the main reason to attend your local church body weekly. If you have no desire to do so, and worshipping with the saints is not a priority for you, is it possible you are not a "true worshipper" as Jesus has defined? A sobering, but necessary, reality check.

Don't be lazy

Some Christians regularly ditch church out of sheer laziness. I know believers who will say, "I was too tired," "I didn't feel like it today," "I had so much to do." These are all lame excuses. The Bible commands believers to "extol the LORD...in the assembly" (Psalm 111:1).

Shunning regular corporate worship of God with the saints is robbing God of His honor. Anemic excuses don't justify such carnal passivity and apathy. On the contrary, the Bible condemns laziness. "As a door turns on its hinges, so a sluggard turns on its bed" (Proverbs 26:14). So don't be a pathetic sluggard—get out of bed and go to church...worship God...give Him His due in light of what He has done for you.

Wrong priorities

Too many Christians skip weekly worship in their local church because of wrong priorities. Worshipping Almighty God, many times, is subservient to other competing goals, like leisure time, the Sunday morning NFL game, sporting events *ad infinitum*, yard work, house chores, getting caught up on work, or even the casual jaunt to Starbucks for morning coffee and relaxation.

A growing trend I have observed in Christian families is parents signing their kids up for sports leagues that compete on Sundays. As a result, corporate worship at church with the saints is sabotaged and neglected for weeks and even months at a time. The spiritual cultivation and nurture for the good of the family is sacrificed on the altar of human aspirations.

I'm an advocate of youth sports leagues. I've been coaching youth for twenty years. I'm an avid basketball enthusiast. Currently I am the head coach for three of my children who compete in city league youth sports leagues. But if the league is going to take away from church life—fellowship and corporate worship—because games and practices are on Wednesdays and Sundays, we simply won't join that league. We'll find another one. God is more of a priority than my son's future NBA career.

Parents are first and foremost models for their children—when they choose sporting activities over worship, they are communicating the wrong priorities to their children during the most impressionable years of their lives. Such parents would do well to learn from Eric Liddell, the world class Olympian who won the gold medal in 1924 in the 400 meter run. He refused to run in an event on Sunday during the Olympics, for that was the Lord's Day. He made God the priority that day—not his own agenda.

Having wrong priorities about church is a real, common, widespread occurrence among Christians today. Jesus reprimanded the church in

Laodicea for having a wrong attitude about God and Christ. Jesus called them "pitiful" (Revelation 3:17) and warned them of imminent rebuke and discipline if they did not change. That warning is issued to the Christians of today as well. Jesus is still watching over and disciplining His church (3:22).

The Priorities of Corporate Worship

The believers of the first Christian church that were in Jerusalem gathered regularly as a corporate body of believers. There were set times when "All the believers were together" (Acts 2:44). This was a practice they were "devoted" to (Acts 2:42). It was their greatest priority in life. It should be ours as well.

We have already seen that the primary objective for the early church when they gathered together was to worship God with a collective voice. But there were other priorities established as well. These priorities are given in Scripture and are prescriptive for the church today. The practice of the early church is our example and model. Some might ask, "What should we be doing as a church body when we gather together each week?" The answer is simply to do what the early church did. Consider their priorities:

Biblical preaching

The Bible says that when the saints came together they "devoted themselves to the apostles' teaching" (Acts 2:42). This refers to the public proclamation of God's Word through systematic preaching and teaching. Preaching God's Word was the hallmark and centerpiece of Jesus' ministry—He was a preacher, not a philanthropist (Matthew 4:17). He preached and taught everywhere He went (Matthew 11:1). He was known as "Rabbi"—which means "Teacher" (John 1:38). Preaching and teaching is what characterized the backbone of the Apostles' ministry as well (Acts 8:4). When they were being sidetracked with menial, cumbersome administrative   duties in the early church, they declared, "It would not be right for us to neglect the ministry of the word of God in order to wait on tables" (Acts 6:2).

Paul commanded Timothy to be devoted "to the public reading of Scripture, to preaching and to teaching. Do not neglect your gift" (1 Timothy 4:13-14). He also charged him to, "Preach the Word; be

31

prepared in season and out of season; correct, rebuke and encourage—with great patience and careful instruction" (2 Timothy 4:2).

God has chosen the mechanism of preaching to communicate His truth (1 Corinthians 1:21). It is through biblical preaching that God saves people (Romans 10:14). It is through preaching the Scriptures that God convicts people of sin and softens their hearts (Matthew 12:41; 1 Corinthians 15:1-2). It is through preaching the Bible that God grows the collective Body of Christ (Colossians 1:28). It is through preaching biblical truth that God exposes false doctrine that leads people astray (2 Corinthians 11:4-7). To neglect the regular, diligent, courageous, systematic, deep, biblical teaching and preaching of the Bible is the greatest abdication of the ministry that a pastor or church could commit.

Go to a church that regularly teaches the Bible. This is one of the main ways that God enables Christians to grow in the faith. If your church is not committed to preaching the Word of God regularly to the gathered body, but has supplanted preaching with story-telling, "relevant" gimmicks, or an assortment of religious business and activities, then pray for your church. Ask God to convict the church leadership about remembering true spiritual priorities for the assembly of believers (Revelation 3:2-3).

Corporate prayer

When the early church gathered together, they prayed together. Corporate prayer was a major priority. Acts says the first Christian church "all joined together constantly in prayer" (1:14). This was a group of about 120 believers. This is what they did at church. Acts 2 says they were "devoted... to prayer" (2:42). Corporate prayer is basic to the true biblical "worship service." When was the last time you went to church and had the opportunity to pray at length with the corporate body of Christ? That rarely happens in many of today's churches. We either don't pray at all or we have the hired clergy say a short prayer for us.

It's more typical that the average Christian goes to church, hears a sermon, maybe throws a little change in the offering plate, and then goes home...never having experienced deep, intimate communication with God through prayer. This must make God sad for His church, for He commanded the church to "always keep on praying for all the saints" (Ephesians 6:18).

If your church is not a praying church; if the leaders are not regularly in prayer for the body and praying with the body; if the saints are not being given regular opportunities to pray, along with fresh teaching on prayer...then your church is in trouble. Pray for your church. Pray for   revival. Ask God to make your local body dependent upon Him for all things. God desires to answer those kinds of prayers, for it is His will that the local church be a praying church (1 Thessalonians 5:17).

Celebrating the Lord's Supper

The Lord's Supper, or "communion," was established by Christ at His Last Supper. "He took bread, gave thanks and broke it, and gave it to them, saying, 'This is my body which is given for you; do this in remembrance of me' " (Luke 22:19). Communion is one of only two ordinances that Christ instituted for the church (the other being baptism).

This ordinance was a priority ministry and form of worship for the early church (Acts 2:42). They practiced it "continually" (Acts 2:42), "on the first day of the week" (Acts 20:7), whenever they "met together" (1 Corinthians 11:18), and "often" (1 Corinthians 11:25-26, KJV). The Lord's Supper was at the heart of early church life and essential to local church ministry.

Sadly today, in many churches that is not the case. The Lord's Supper has been minimized, forgotten or relegated to the status of an occasional religious exercise performed all too infrequently, or at inconvenient times when large portions of the local body are missing. A Christian friend recently told me that his church does not have communion at all. The reason, he said, was that the leadership decided that communion was just too divisive, so they eliminated it altogether!

This is shameful in light of Jesus' passion for this ordinance. Jesus testified, "With fervent desire I have desired to eat this Passover with you before I suffer" (Luke 22:15). Contrast that statement with many Christians' apathetic, nonchalant and perfunctory attitude toward communion today. Believers need to be regularly reminded of the primary significance and meaning of the Lord's Supper so that it is reinstated to its rightful place of importance in the local church.

Make a habit of regularly celebrating the Lord's Supper by taking communion. It's one of the most tangible ways we can have fellowship with God, remembering His death on our behalf while waiting in expectation for His glorious return in the future (1 Corinthians 11:26).

Remember the basics

In review, we have seen that the early church had basic priorities when they regularly met as the collective body of Christ. The main components of their weekly worship service included corporate worship of God, biblical preaching and teaching, praying together as a body, and celebrating the Lord's Supper. It's that simple. Christians and churches that deviate from that pattern are departing from the New Testament model to their own detriment.

Go to Worship on the Lord's Day

There is biblical evidence suggesting that the early church set aside a regular day during the week for corporate worship. This would have been very natural for the first Christians, who were Jewish. The Jews already had an established routine of observing one day a week that was dedicated to God. For Old Testament Jews that day was the "Sabbath" or Saturday—the seventh day of the week. For the early church that day eventually became the first day of the week, which came to be known as the "Lord's Day."

Jesus rose from the dead on Sunday, the first day of the week (Luke 24:1-8). It was on the first day of the week that the church was born when the Holy Spirit was poured out on the first followers of Christ (Acts 2). It was on the first day of the week that Paul commanded the early churches to practice corporate almsgiving as a religious duty (1 Corinthians 16:1-3). It was on the first day of the week—Sunday—that Paul led a corporate worship service with believers, having communion and Bible teaching in a formal setting (Acts 20:7-12).

By the time John wrote Revelation, in the 90's, Sunday had come to be known by the church simply as "the Lord's day" (Revelation 1:10), for it eventually became the universally designated day when the saints collectively gathered to worship God and to weekly celebrate the resurrection of Christ.

It is clear that God wants the church to gather as a group regularly for corporate worship. Paul's entire discussion in 1 Corinthians 11-14 is given for providing guidelines and proper decorum for the regular public assembly of the church. The believers were expected to "come together as a church" (11:18) for collective prayer (11:4-5), to celebrate the Lord's death and resurrection (11:17-26), to exercise the spiritual gifts for mutual edification (12:1-30), spiritual instruction (14:6), to praise God (14:16), and to worship God (14:25). And the day set aside for those biblical priorities was the Lord's Day—the first day of the week.

If you are a Christian, make a priority of setting aside Sunday as a day to focus on Christ through corporate worship, spiritual fellowship and service with other believers in your local church. Be obedient to Him. Make God your number one priority. Heed His exhortation to us when He said,

> *Let us hold unswervingly to the hope we profess, for he who promised is faithful. And let us consider how we may spur one another on toward love and good deeds. Let us not give up meeting together, as some are in the habit of doing, but let us encourage one another—and all the more as you see the Day approaching (Hebrews 10:23-25).*

Questions for Review

1. In a few sentences, write your own definition of biblical worship:

_____

_____

_____

_____

2. Today, who is eligible to become a priest and a saint? How does one become either?

_____

_____

_____

_____

3. What did Jesus mean when He referred to Himself as "I AM"?

_____

_____

_____

_____

4. How can Christianity worship Jesus and the Father and still be a monotheistic religion?

_____

_____

_____

5. Give a biblical definition of the Trinity:

_____

_____

_____

6. Define the "New Covenant" and give key Bible verses that explain it:

_____

_____

_____

7. What is the main reason Christians should go to church? Give a verse to support your answer:

_____

_____

_____

8. Why is biblical preaching a priority for the gathered local church?

_____

_____

_____

9. How often do you have communion? When was the last time? Is it a regular priority in your life?

_____

_____

_____

10. Have you set aside Sunday as the Lord's Day? Do you regularly worship God with the local church on the first day of the week? If not, how can you make it a priority?

_____

_____

_____

For further study on *Worship!* **see these helpful resources:**
The Wonder of Worship, by Ronald Allen
Nine Marks of a Healthy Church, by Mark Dever
Worship in Spirit and Truth, by John Frame
A Better Way, by Michael Horton
Disciplines of a Godly Man, by R. Kent Hughes
The Ultimate Priority, by John MacArthur
Knowing God, by J. I. Packer
Desiring God, by John Piper
The Pursuit of God, by A. W. Tozer
Spiritual Disciplines Within the Church, by Donald Whitney
Real Worship, by Warren Wiersbe

2

Fellowship!

"they devoted themselves to...fellowship...
All the believers were together
and had everything in common"
(Acts 2:42, 44)

When the church was born on the Day of Pentecost 2,000 years ago, the early believers committed themselves to a few key priorities. Acts 2:42 says "fellowship" was one of them. So "fellowship" is literally a birthmark of the Christian church, and should be common practice in the life of every follower of Christ. Consider below the following highlights of what the Bible has to say about the practice of Christian fellowship.

What is Fellowship?

The New Testament word for "fellowship" is *koinonia* (pronounced 'coy-no-KNEE-ah'). This is a beautifully rich, colorful and vigorous word from the Greek language. It is used frequently in the Christian community. There's a church called 'Koinonia Fellowship,' a web-site called 'Koinonia House,' a Christian music group called 'Koinonia' as well as schools, colleges and seminaries that go by the same name.

The word *koinonia* is translated in various ways in the New Testament depending on the context. For example it is rendered as "fellowship" (Philippians 2:1), "partnership" (Philippians 1:5), "contribution" (Romans 15:26) or even "communion". But at the very heart of the word *koinonia* is the concept of *sharing*. And that is how it is translated in several passages (i.e., 2 Corinthians 8:4; Philemon 6; Hebrews 13:16). That is the essence of what Christian fellowship is—it is sharing. Christian fellowship is mutual sharing at the most intimate level, in all areas of life, as a result of the transforming work of God in the life of an individual.

In secular Greek *koinonia* was used in reference to those who held joint ownership in a business venture or a legal transaction. The New Testament writers infused the term with religious overtones to describe all the spiritual rights and privileges that belong to individual Christians by virtue of their identity in Christ. Everything that belongs to Christ, He willingly imparts and shares with His followers who have been adopted into His spiritual family through personal salvation. A Christian shares in Christ's suffering (Philippians 3:10), death (Romans 6:3), resurrection from the dead (Romans 6:5), inheritance (Romans 8:17), and His future reign in glory (2 Timothy 2:12). And every Christian shares a common spiritual foundation with every other Christian by virtue of a personal relationship with Jesus Christ—all Christians are in God's spiritual family.

So when the Book of Acts says that the early believers were devoted to "fellowship," it means that they mutually shared their lives with each other because of their common relationship to Jesus Christ as their Savior and God as their Father. In the same way, all Christians today are called to have fellowship with other Christians—to share their lives with others. Neglecting fellowship with other Christians is disobedient and will stunt spiritual development.

God is the Model of Fellowship

According to the Bible, God is triune; He eternally exists as one God who has three distinct Persons—Father, Son and Holy Spirit. The three Persons of the Trinity are co-equal and co-eternal. They have always existed and are uncreated. And the Bible says that from eternity past they have always enjoyed sweet fellowship with one another, even before creation.

In John 17:5 Jesus prayed to the Father saying, "And now, Father, glorify me in your presence with the glory I had with you before the world began." Here Jesus makes it clear that before His incarnation He existed with the Father in a glorious relationship before the world was created. The nature of that relationship was personal, intimate communion.

John 1:1 says that in the beginning (before creation) Jesus (the Word) was "with" God the Father. The Greek word for "with" in that verse can literally be translated as "toward" and is a picture of Jesus being face-to-face with the Father before creation. Being face-to-face with someone speaks of equality, communion, and the most intimate kind of fellowship with another person. And that was the nature of Christ's fellowship with the Father since before creation.

Jesus further said, "I am in the Father and the Father is in me" (John 14:11) and "I and the Father are one" (John 10:30). In some mysterious, supernatural, inexplicable manner, Jesus has existed for all eternity in constant fellowship with the Father.

This is also true with respect to the Holy Spirit, who has also been in constant eternal fellowship with the Father and the Son. Jesus said that the Holy Spirit presides with the Father in heaven and proceeds from the Father (John 15:26). The Holy Spirit was with the Father and the Son at the time of creation (Genesis 1:2) and is in constant, inseparable fellowship with them (Psalm 139:7-8). The testimony of Scripture is that God the Father, God the Son, and God the Holy Spirit co-exist in constant, intimate, eternal fellowship with one another.

We were Created for Fellowship

The Bible says that humans were created in God's image. That means that we were made with attributes and characteristics that are similar to those of the Creator. First and foremost that means that we are "persons." As persons we possess reason, choice, morals, and spirituality among other traits that make us distinct from the rest of creation, like inanimate objects, plants and animals.

Another significant example of being made in God's image and after His likeness, is that humans were created for fellowship; we need community and companionship. Humans cannot live in isolation—we are inherently social beings. Just as God has eternally existed as three distinct Persons who have enjoyed heavenly fellowship and intimacy with one another, God's design for people is that they live in fellowship and intimacy with others as well.

This is clear from Genesis at the time of creation when God created the first two people. When the triune God decided to create humanity He declared, "Let us make man in our image, in our likeness...So God created man in his own image, in the image of God he created him; male and female he created them" (1:26-27). Notice that humanity most fully reflects the image of God with a man and a woman together—two people together, in intimate fellowship.

The creation account goes on to say that in the beginning it was not good for the man, Adam, to be all alone (2:18). He would be completed—fully reflecting God's image—only after being united with his wife, Eve. Together, as man and wife in fellowship and communion with one another (as "one flesh"), they would fully reflect the plural nature of God's being (2:24). God is a social being, and because we were made in His image, we also are social beings. As such, we were created for fellowship. It is in our very nature.

Fellowship with Your Local Church

Because we are social beings, created for fellowship, our spiritual growth and development are in large measure contingent upon our commitment to the local church. Fellowship with other Christians is a catalyst for spiritual nurture and health. That's why the Bible commands Christians not to neglect fellowship in the local church: "Let us not give up meeting together, as some are in the habit of doing" (Hebrews 10:25).

If you want to stunt your spiritual growth, then just cut yourself off from regular fellowship with other Christians. God doesn't want any *Lone Ranger* Christians. We can't live fruitful lives in isolation. Ecclesiastes puts it this way:

> *Two are better than one, because they have a good return for their work: If one falls down, his friend can help him up. But pity the man who falls and has no one to help him up! Also, if two lie down together, they will keep warm. But how can one keep warm alone? Though one may be overpowered, two can defend themselves. A cord of three strands is not quickly broken (4:9-12).*

God expects Christians to be in fellowship with each other, sharing their lives together in close proximity, with vulnerability and sincerity. By design, God will grow His church to maturity as His believers mutually live in community together, ministering to one another as a corporate entity. That is what Paul said in Ephesians. Every Christian needs to be an active part in the church community to bring about corporate edification: "From him [Christ, the Head of the Body] the whole body, joined and held together by every supporting ligament, grows and builds itself up in love, as each part does its work" (4:16). In this passage, "every supporting ligament" refers to every Christian.

Fellowship entails give-and-take relationships. It requires mutual commitment and accountability with others. It means walking through life together with other saints. It means cultivating deep, transparent spiritual friendships with other believers. True Christian fellowship is interdependent living on the spiritual plane. Fellowship means being a regular, functional, contributing part of a local church community. The first Christians invested in fellowship in many ways including the following:

- studying the Bible together
- praying with and for other believers
- talking about spiritual things with each other
- confessing sins to other Christians
- celebrating the Lord's Supper with other saints
- observing baptisms together
- worshipping God with the people of God
- singing praises to God with other Christians
- weeping with others and sharing life's trials
- rejoicing with others
- interacting with other Christian families
- helping each other as needs would arise
- sharing meals together

The world encourages people to live for "self." Christian fellowship is just the opposite. It is a worldview that is "other-oriented." The New Testament is replete with commands for Christians to minister to "one another" in various ways. To do so is to fulfill Christian fellowship. Consider some of the main "one anothers" that the church is to obey.

Love one another

Jesus said to His disciples, "Love one another. As I have loved you, so you must love one another. By this all men will know that you are my disciples, if you love one another" (John 13:34-35). If you are a Christian, it will be obvious by how you treat other Christians. That's what Jesus said.

The word 'love' in the New Testament is primarily an action, not a sentimental feeling. John 3:16 says that "God so loved" that He "gave." Giving to others is the essence of true love.

Biblical love is also selfless and sacrificial. In John 15:13 Jesus said, "Greater love has no one than this, that he lay down his life for his friends." Jesus was saying that love is shown by being willing to die for someone else if necessary. Love is not just good intentions or nice words— love is not true love until it is put into action.

True love is also supernatural—it's not natural. Biblical love comes from God, we are not born with it. The Bible says "love comes from God" (1 John 4:7). People who are not born again (those who are not true believers in Christ), do not possess this kind of supernatural love (1 John 4:8-9). Supernatural, heavenly love is received the moment someone becomes a Christian (Romans 5:5). At that point the Holy Spirit begins to live in the believer and He produces love in the Christian's heart (Galatians 5:22). So every true born-again believer has the reservoir of God's love at his or her disposal. All Christians have the capacity to truly love as Jesus loved. There are no excuses.

With respect to fellowship, Christians need to love others in the church by living lives of selfless, sacrificial, supernatural giving. This might entail giving money, food, help, time, or a place to sleep. The early Christians were exemplary in this way:

> All the believers were one in heart and mind. No one claimed that any of his possessions was his own, but they shared everything they had....There were no needy persons among them. For from time to time those who owned lands or houses sold them, brought the money from the sales and put it at the apostles' feet, and it was distributed to anyone as he had need. (Acts 4:32, 34-35).

Serve one another

Christian fellowship entails serving others. Galatians 5:13 commands believers to "serve one another in love." Serving others means waiting on them and attending to their needs.

This is why Jesus came down from heaven to this fallen world—to serve others. He said about Himself, "For even the Son of Man did not come to be served, but to serve, and to give his life as a ransom for many" (Mark 10:45). Jesus also said, "Now that I, your Lord and Teacher, have washed your feet, you also should wash one another's feet" (John 13:14). In Jesus' day, it was customary for the lowliest slave in a house to wash the guests' feet as they entered the house. It was a menial, practical, humble, smelly duty. And on the night before His death, Jesus washed His disciples' dirty feet just before His Last Supper. He was committed to serving others.

Serving others is a hallmark of the Christian ethic. The world says that to be a great leader, you must rule over others. Jesus said just the opposite. A great leader is one who serves others (Matthew 20:25-28).

Over the years I have been the recipient of Christians serving me countless times. I remember a while back when I moved to work at a church in Utah. On the day that my family arrived, after driving our moving truck for hours and hours, we were wiped out. The thought of unloading the truck and unpacking was dreadful. Then to our delight, as we arrived at our new home, we were greeted by about twenty people from our new church (mostly teenagers from the youth group), who were young, strong, fresh and ready to unload our truck for us. And they did—in less than thirty minutes. We did not even know who these people were, but they were fellow believers from the church where we were about to serve. We were blessed by modern day Christians living out the biblical mandate that calls believers to "serve one another in love"!

Encourage one another

Words have power. Proverbs says, "An anxious heart weighs a man down, but a kind word cheers him up" (12:25). An encouraging word spoken at just the right time can lift the spirit in a unique way. The Christian community is supposed to be a place where people are given to verbally encouraging each other on a regular basis.

The Bible says, "encourage one another and build each other up" (1 Thessalonians 5:11). The word for "encourage" here means "to speak comforting words." And the word for "build up" means "to edify—to speak constructive words."

The Christian community should be a place where believers can be regularly comforted and built up with edifying words. What a contrast from the world where speech is routinely caustic, sarcastic, cynical, biting and negative. TV shows are rife with crude humor that is typified by "cut-downs" that are supposed to be funny. A joke or a punch-line at the expense of someone else's reputation is not funny, appropriate or biblical, no matter the intent. The Bible says "to build up" not "cut down."

How often have you heard someone make fun of someone else, offend that person, and then later justify the godless speech by saying, "Oh, I was just kidding"? Compare that with what God expects from the mouth of a Christian: "Do not let any unwholesome talk come out of your mouths, but only what is helpful for building others up according to their needs, that it may benefit those who listen...But among you there must not even be a hint of...obscenity, foolish talk or coarse joking, which are out of place, but rather thanksgiving" (Ephesians 4:29; 5:3-4). The word for "unwholesome" in this passage literally means "rotten" or "spoiled" as in rotten fruit or spoiled meat—both of which stink. In contrast to "rotten" words, Paul says the Christian should speak words that "build up." The word for "build up" here is a graphic compound Greek word that means "to construct a house." The point of the passage is that believers should not tear each other down with sarcastic, biting, insulting speech—even when it is done in jest. Rather believers are commanded to routinely build each other up with encouraging words as a matter of routine. Colossians 4:6 states it this way: "Let your conversation be always full of grace, seasoned with salt, so that you may know how to answer everyone."

It's embarrassing and even shameful to think about how many Christians have allowed the world's sour and poisoned speech to influence their conversation in this manner. How are you doing with your words and everyday speech? We all need to take inventory and ask the Holy Spirit to examine us. Are you routinely sarcastic and cynical? Do you tell or are you entertained by off-color, rude or inappropriate jokes? Do you demean others, even your friends to get a laugh, and then justify it by saying, "I was just kidding"? Do you boast about how great you are and how you excel above all the rest to gain a timely laugh? We can all be convicted by such diagnostic questions. After all, James says it is impossible for sinners to always keep their tongues and lips in check (3:2). Nevertheless, our desire should be to always try to please God in all that we do, even if we fail at times (1 Corinthians 10:31).

Stem the tide, go against the flow, be different and begin making "encouraging words" a normal part of your verbal arsenal. After all, Jesus warned us that we will be held accountable for how we talk to people in this life:

> But I tell you that men will have to give an account on the day of judgment for every careless word they have spoken. For by your words you will be acquitted, and by your words you will be condemned (Matthew 12:36-37).

Instruct one another

Colossians 3:16 says Christians should "teach and admonish one another." This means Christians should *counsel* one another. That is what these two words mean—"teach" and "admonish." *Teach* is the positive aspect of counseling and *admonish* is the negative aspect of counseling. These two words refer to giving verbal, didactic instruction to another—communicating propositional truth directed at the mind, with the goal of changing the heart and the behavior. It is akin to the verse that commands believers to "speak the truth in love" (Ephesians 4:15).

What are Christians supposed to be teaching and admonishing each other with? According to the first part of Colossians 3:16, it's "the word of Christ" or biblical truth. We are to counsel each other with the Bible—the content of God's Word. This makes sense, for the Bible is God's truth and is sufficient to deal with all of life's issues (2 Timothy 3:16-17; 2 Peter 1:3). The Bible is alive, authoritative, inerrant, sufficient, relevant, and supernatural (Hebrews 4:12). Jesus said the Bible is God's Word and the truth (John 17:17).

Jesus also said, "know the truth and the truth will set you free" (John 8:32). Part of Christian fellowship is getting godly counsel—the truth—and giving godly counsel to others on a regular basis. The Bible says there is wisdom in a multitude of counselors (Proverbs 15:22). God wants His people to speak the truth to each other so they can make wise decisions in daily living.

All Christians have the Holy Spirit of Truth living inside of them—the resident personal Teacher (1 John 2:27; 4:4). God's truth for life is at the disposal of every believer. When you have an important decision to make, or need practical wisdom, insight or advice—then do what God commands. Get wisdom from a multitude of godly counselors. And pray for God's discernment. God promises to impart wisdom under such conditions (Proverbs 3:5-8; James 1:5-8).

Unfortunately, today too many Christians are seeking counsel from the wrong sources. They flock to people like Dr. Laura, Dr. Phil, and countless other popular, secular self-help gurus, who are not even Christians. Worse still, Christians are flocking to secular, but "professional," psychologists, psychiatrists and therapists, without even considering the fellowship of the church as a resource of supernatural, heavenly wisdom.

The Bible calls Jesus the "Wonderful Counselor" (Isaiah 9:6). Jesus called the Holy Spirit the "Counselor" (John 15:26). Isaiah refers to God as the incomparable "counselor" (40:13). And the Scripture refers to spirit-filled Christians as competent, capable counselors (Romans 15:14) by virtue of their salvation and relationship to Almighty God (Ephesians 1:3-9). It's time for the church to look to the fellowship of the church, which is the pillar of God's truth (1 Timothy 3:15), for the answers and wisdom for life's problems.

Fellowship with Believers

Should Christians fellowship with unbelievers and if so in what manner is this possible? Well, according to the Bible, this is not possible. Paul emphatically addressed this issue with the Corinthians. He told them point- blank that they were not to be "unequally yoked" with unbelievers. With a flurry of rhetorical questions he clarified what he meant by this prohibition:

> Do not be yoked together with unbelievers. For what do righteousness and wickedness have in common? Or what fellowship can light have with darkness? What harmony is there between Christ and Belial? What does a believer have in common with an unbeliever? What agreement is there between the

temple of God and idols? For we are the temple of the living God...."Therefore come out from them and be separate," says the Lord (2 Corinthians 6:14-17).

In this passage Paul is contrasting Christians with non-Christians. He clearly shows that believers have no spiritual or religious common ground with unbelievers. He refers to Christians with the titles "righteousness," "light," "Christ," "believer," and "the temple of God." Notice how he portrays unbelievers—they are "wickedness," "darkness," "Belial" (a name for *Satan*, the devil), "unbeliever," and "idols." He could not have made a stronger contrast between the two categories of people.

John the Apostle also made an absolute antithesis between believers and unbelievers. He said, "Who is the liar? It is the man who denies that Jesus is the Christ. Such a man is the antichrist—he denies the Father and the Son...do not let anyone lead you astray. He who does what is right is righteous, just as he [Jesus] is righteous. He who does what is sinful is of the devil, because the devil has been sinning from the beginning" (1 John 2:22; 3:7-8). Notice that John says unbelievers are "of the devil." That's very harsh language—hardly politically correct or diplomatic.

Jesus made the same kind of dramatic spiritual diagnosis as well. To the Jews who denied that Jesus was God incarnate, the Old Testament Messiah, and the only Savior of the world, Jesus said, "You belong to your father the devil, and you want to carry out your father's desire. He was a murderer from the beginning, not holding to the truth, for there is no truth in him" (John 8:44). Jesus told unbelievers that their father was "the devil"—not a way to win friends and influence people! But it was the truth nonetheless.

The Apostle Paul, the Apostle John and the Lord Jesus all make the same assessment: unbelievers are servants of Satan, filled with sinful desires and reject the truth of God. The main truth unbelievers reject is the truth about who Jesus is. They deny that Jesus is eternal, the Creator, worthy of worship, full deity, the only Savior and equal to the Father. This is the nexus of what sets believers apart from unbelievers—believing the truth about who Jesus is and relating to Him accordingly.

Anyone who believes the right things about Jesus and knows Him personally is a true Christian, is in the family of God and has the Holy Spirit living inside. This is true of every believer. And this is the basis by which we can enjoy true fellowship with one another. All believers share in the same spiritual life that God imparts to those who know Jesus. Unbelievers don't have that spiritual life, so there can be no real fellowship or communion between Christians and non-Christians. As Paul said in 2 Corinthians 6, there is nothing believers have in common with unbelievers when it comes to spiritual realities. Therefore, he says, "do not be unequally yoked with unbelievers."

Despite this truth, there are a growing number of Evangelical Christians today who are yoking up with non-Christians in various illegitimate ways. More and more churches are inviting unbelievers to take part and even lead in various aspects of the weekly worship service in the local church. How can unbelievers encourage others to worship and praise God when they don't even know God? It defies reason, but it goes on constantly. The justification often sounds like this: "Well, if we can just get them in the church building, doing whatever, then maybe we can reach them with the gospel." That's a sincere desire, but it is sincerely misguided and unbiblical.

God has made it clear that the public, corporate worship of the saints in church is to be led by those who are spiritually called, mature and qualified and that all things are to be done decently and in order (1 Timothy 2-3; 1 Corinthians 14). Unbelievers should not be encouraged to serve, pray, lead, sing to God, take the Lord's Supper, preach, teach or do anything else that usurps the rights and privileges that belong only to Christians. To do otherwise merely confounds the issue, gives unbelievers a false sense of acceptance before a holy God, illegitimately relieves believers of their mandate to go into the world to evangelize the lost, and dilutes the pure worship of God that He deserves and desires from His people.

It is clear, then, that Christians cannot have spiritual fellowship with unbelievers. Instead of trying to subtly trick non-Christians into acting, thinking, talking and associating like Christians through osmosis, believers need to draw clear boundaries between themselves and the world. And instead of engaging in a superficial co-allegiance to a generic belief in God with unbelievers, Christians need to aggressively infiltrate the world (not let unbelievers infiltrate the church), evangelize the lost, model godliness, unify with real believers, and pray for the salvation of unbelievers so they, too, can become a legitimate part of Christian fellowship that comes only through knowing Jesus Christ personally.

You Better Get Used to It!

One of the main reasons God has us here in this life is to prepare us for eternity in heaven. The fate of a believer upon death is instant heaven. In heaven, the perfected believer will be in the company of the Lord Jesus, God the Father, the Holy Spirit and all the saints who have ever lived (not to mention a gazillion angels everywhere).

Regarding the massive group of believers that will live in heaven, the Bible describes them as "a great multitude that no one could count, from every nation, tribe, people and language" (Revelation 7:9). Daniel describes the saints in heaven as being innumerable—or, too many to count, humanly speaking (Daniel 7). That's a lot of people!

Apparently, some professing Christians don't like people. They have an aversion to crowds and large numbers of warm-blooded, born-again Homosapiens. They prefer isolation, seclusion and the cloistered life. But heaven won't be like that. There's no agoraphobia in heaven.

God's perfect design is that believers mingle, interact, and fellowship with each other in vibrant, dynamic, ongoing ways. That's how it's going to be in eternity. There won't be any place to hide. But, apparently, we won't have reason to hide then, nor will we want to. We will willingly, freely live in exuberant fellowship with God and all the saints when we get to heaven. So we might as well start practicing now in this life to get used to it.

Questions for Review

1. Write a biblical definition for "fellowship." What is the Greek word for "fellowship"?

_____

_____

_____

_____

2. In what way does John 1:1 explain the nature of Jesus' fellowship with the Father?

_____

_____

_____

_____

3. God created humans as social beings, created for fellowship. How does that relate to being made in God's image?

_____

_____

_____

_____

4. Give a Bible verse that speaks of the importance of being involved in fellowship with others.

_____

_____

_____

_____

5. What were some of the main ways the early disciples had fellowship with one another?

_____

_____

_____

_____

6. How should Christians speak to one another in light of 1 Thessalonians 5:11? How should they not speak?

_____

_____

_____

_____

7. When is it okay to seek counsel from those who are not Christians? When is it not okay? What are the boundaries for determining this?

_____

_____

_____

_____

8. What should our relationship be with unbelievers in light of 2 Corinthians 6:14-17? What does Paul mean when he says a believer cannot have fellowship with an unbeliever?

_____

_____

_____

_____

9. Is regular, ongoing, consistent fellowship with believers in the local church a priority for you right now? Why or why not?

_____

_____

_____

_____

10. If someone is "shy" or an "introvert," are they exempt from being actively involved in biblical fellowship? What are some suggestions you might give to a Christian who struggles with this issue?

_____

_____

_____

_____

For further study on *Fellowship!* **see these helpful resources:**
Competent to Counsel, by Jay Adams
Building Up One Another, by Gene Getz
Encouraging One Another, by Gene Getz
Loving One Another, by Gene Getz
Serving One Another, by Gene Getz
The Transforming Community, by Mark Lauterbach
We Belong Together, by Bruce Milne
War of Words, by Paul David Tripp

3

Join!

"No one who puts his hand to the plow
and looks back is fit for service
in the kingdom of God"
(Luke 9:62)

The above quotation is from the Lord Jesus Himself. He spoke these words to warn certain disciples who expressed apparent interest in following Him. He was telling them that if they were going to follow Him, then they needed to make a deliberate, formal commitment to join Him—with no looking back. Jesus established and maintained a high standard of accountability for His followers and that standard remains today in His Church.

The early church that Jesus' apostles established had a definitive local church membership pattern. In the early church, if you became a Christian then you immediatley joined the local assembly of believers. And you joined in a formal, accountable, long-term manner.

Today it is commonplace for Christians to go to church, but to never become formal members of any local body. Countless Christians the world over never "join" the church and many are even passionatley averse to such a notion. Many others engage in "church-hopping." This is when Christians sporadically go to various churches, buffet style, picking and choosing what they like from all the different options, but coming short of ever committing to and identifying with one particular local body in any long-term manner. Many times the mindset is, "what will this church do for me—how can my needs and desires be fulfilled."

That is sad but true. Nevertheless, the Bible clearly teaches that if you are a saved, born-again Christian, then God wants you to formally join a Bible-believing church. He wants you to become a local church member. Let's survey some of the most basic truths on this matter from the New Testament.

Jesus Taught Church Membership

One of the New Testament metaphors describing the church is "flock" (Acts 20:28), which means the people are depicted as the "sheep" (John 21:16) and the leaders are portrayed as "shepherds" or "pastors." Jesus was the Master Shepherd (1 Peter 5:4). As such He's the ultimate authority when it comes to discussing the business of the church.

Jesus once told a parable to illustrate the nature of true spiritual care and leadership. He said,

> *Suppose one of you has a hundred sheep and loses one of them. Does he not leave the ninety-nine in the open country and go after the lost sheep until he finds it? And when he finds it, he joyfully puts it on his shoulders and goes home (Luke 15:4-6).*

One basic truth flowing from Jesus' parable is that any responsible shepherd will have a definitive number of members in his flock. The good shepherd knows all of his sheep by name. There is a finite, formal membership to his flock for which he is responsible and accountable. The faithful pastor, like Jesus above, knows exactly who belongs to his fold. This is only possible if there is a definite membership.

Jesus said in John 10 that the Good Shepherd "calls his own sheep by name" (v. 3). Notice, they are called his "own"—the sheep belong somewhere...there's a definite affiliation. And because they are members this allows the pastor to "know them by name." If you don't join a church and become a full-fledged, accountable member, then how is the local church leadership supposed to know you by name and thus protect, provide, nurture, teach and lead you as one of Christ's sheep? It's ultimately impossible.

Church Membership is the New Testament Model
It was in the First Church of Jerusalem

The next thing to consider is that church membership is the biblical model. That is clear from the book of Acts, which chronicles the birth and growth of the first church in Jerusalem. The first church began in Jerusalem on the Day of Pentecost (Acts 2:1) when the Holy Spirit came down from heaven and took up residence in the first believers.

This church began with "a group numbering about a hundred and twenty" people (Acts 1:15). The fact that the Bible gives a specific number of people is significant. It means that someone in charge was keeping a formal head count of who constituted the First Church of Jerusalem. There were clearly identifiable members. Names are even mentioned in Acts 1:13-14.

This pattern continues through Acts as the early church continued to grow. Luke, the author of Acts, gives repeated updates of how many people were members of the church. Someone was counting heads and writing this important information down in the church ledger.

For example, on the Day of Pentecost, Peter preached a powerful evangelistic sermon to thousands of people out on the streets of Jerusalem. Many were convicted of the truth and believed in the gospel. Luke says that "three-thousand were added" to the church that day (Acts 2:41). The word for "added" (*prostithemi*) here is a very specific compound Greek word meaning "placed into" and speaks of a deliberate, calculated act of adding a select number to a greater, existing whole. In other words, the early church was keeping a careful count of those who were being added as new members to the body.

People continued to formally join the church at Jerusalem after the Day of Pentecost, for in Acts 2:47 Luke says, "the Lord *added* to their number daily those who were being saved." The head count continued as the church grew and grew. The church flourished even more and mushroomed to the point where "the number of men grew to about five thousand"! (Acts 4:4).

The word for "number" here is the word *arithmos* from which we get "arithmetic"—the science of the computation of numbers. The early church was scientific in its calculation as to who was joining the church. There was no willy-nilly, informal, loosey-goosey, superficial affiliation on the part of the first Christians when it came to joining a church.

Christians didn't church hop from one congregation to the next, eschewing any formal commitment to membership based on personal convenience or the latest preference. Church membership was taken seriously and considered a privilege.

Acts 5:14 goes on to say that "more and more men and women believed in the Lord and were **added** to their number." These people were "added" to the church by "joining" the church according to Acts 5:13. The word for "join" there means "to formally join" or "to unite with—to be glued together".

This same word is used in 1 Corinthians 6:16 when describing a man and a woman being "joined together" through sexual intimacy. It is also used to describe the relationship between a believer and Christ when they are "joined together" at the point of salvation (1 Corinthians 6:17). So this word "added" is the strongest word-picture possible to describe a formal, intimate, inextricable joining of two parties entering a mutual relationship of the highest commitment. This is what the first Christians did—they "joined" the local church in Jerusalem as formal, "baptized," identifiable members!

According to the Apostle Paul

Paul was an apostle and church planter. He started many churches from scratch and trained up leadership in those churches to lead them when he departed. A definite number of people composed these churches. When he wrote letters to these churches, it was common for him to designate the church memebership with specificity (Philippians 1:1). In all his letters he names specific people in each local church (Romans 16:1-24; 1 Corinthians 1:14; Ephesians 6:21; Philippians 4:2; Colossians 4:7-18; 1 Thessalonians 3:2; 1 Timothy 1:20; 2 Timothy 4:9-21). He wasn't just addressing some obtuse, nameless mass of humanity generically clustered in disparate   locations. He wrote with authority, always expecting full compliance on behalf of his listeners. He could do so because he was writing to specific people, with names and faces, who were definite members in the local churches he worked with. This would only have been possible if there was a formal membership kept in the local churches.

Paul instructed Timothy to keep a "widow's list" at the church in Ephesus (1 Tmothy 5:3, 9-11). This was a formal ledger of women's names in that specific congregation who qualified for special care in that church. If there was no formal church membership, no possible widow's list could have been maintained.

Keeping a formal ledger of church members would have been quite natural for Paul who was an ex-Pharisee and a former high ranking member of the Jewish Sanhedrin. The Jews in Paul's day had religious services and gatherings in a place called the synagogue. Jesus even attended and taught in the synagogue (Luke 4:14-15). The early church modeled some of their religious practices after the synagogue (Acts 13:13 ff.; 15:21). To be a part of a synagogue you had to be a formal member. There were qualifications for joining and when you got kicked out, or your formal membership was revoked, you were said to be "unsynagogued" (John 9:22). So formal membership in local places of religious practice was the norm in Paul's day. To expect the same standard in the local church assemblies would have been natural for the Apostle.

Church Membership is Required of Church Leaders

In 1 Peter 5 God commands church leaders to require a formal church membership in the local assembly. God gives this imperative through one of the first local church pastors, Peter the Apostle. Peter writes,

> *To the elders among you, I appeal as a fellow elder...Be shepherds of God's flock that is under your care, serving as overseers—not because you must, but because you are willing, as God wants you to be; not greedy for money, but eager to serve, not lording it over those entrusted to you, but being examples to the flock. And when the Chief Shepherd appears, you will receive the crown of glory that will never fade away (vv.1-4).*

This passage highlights the importance of formal church membership in the local assembly. For example, in this text Peter is talking to pastors, or "elders"—those who are in charge of the local church. Here he tells them that local pastors are responsible for the people in the flock who "are under your care." That means there is a definite number of people for which pastors are responsible. The Greek literally says, "shepherd the flock of God among you."

The local church pastor can fulfill this obligation only if he knows exactly what people are in his flock—and the only way to establish that is through formal church membership. Just like in Jesus' parable earlier— He knew there were exactly one hundred sheep in His fold, and He even knew them by name.

Peter gets even more specific when he refers to those church members who are "entrusted to you" (verse 3). The phrase "those entrusted" literally is "the specific ones alloted to you." It is a finite number of people who are considered a stewardship responsibility given by God to each local church.

And at the judgment God is going to require an inventory of how church leaders treated every member in their respective churches. So the onus is on local pastors to get to know every person in their churches and ensure that they become formal members so they can be cared for properly. For this to happen, formal church membership is a prerequisite.

A corollary passage to the above truth is in Hebrews 13:17. It reads: "Obey your [church] leaders and submit to their authority. They keep watch over you as men who must give an account. Obey them so that their work will be a joy, not a burden, for that would be of no advantage to you." The writer here is talking to Christians in the local church. The commands given here for the church leaders and the people in the local assembly could not be fulfilled without formal church membership.

As a local church pastor I am commanded here to make sure those I am responsible for submit to church authority. But if someone is not a formal church member under my local jurisdiction then how can I enforce such an imperative? Moreover, if someone in the congregation refuses to become a church member then why should they have to "obey" and "submit" to any of the leaders in any given local church? They could simply shrug off such binding accountability at any time with the retort, "I don't have to do what they tell me—I'm not a member at that church!"

Unfortunately, I have seen just that happen all too many times in the ministry. Such a cavalier attitude on the part of any foot-loose and fancy-free Christian is not good. It is actually defiance—disobedience to God's Word. And the end result for such a professing believer is just as the Hebrews author said—"it is no advantage to you"—meaning God will deal with such sinister behavior in one way or another (Galatians 6:7).

Church Discipline Requires Church Membership

In the four Gospels Jesus made reference to the "church" by name only twice. Both of those instances are in Matthew. The first one was the prediction or prophecy whereby He promised to build His church (16:18). The second instance is the time where He told His disciples how to ensure the healthy maintenance of His church by employing church discipline. Jesus put a premium on maintaining healthy relationships among people, and His divine strategy for doing so is delineated in Matthew 18:15-17:

> *If your brother sins against you, go and show him his fault, just between the two of you. If he listens to you, you have won your brother over. But if he will not listen, take one or two others along, so that "every matter may be established by the testimony of two or three witnesses." If he refuses to listen to them, tell it to the church; and if he refuses to listen even to the church, treat him even as you would a pagan or a tax collector.*

Throughout church history this passage has rightly been referred to as the "church discipline process." When sin arises in the church this procedure is the guideline of how to confront sin with the goal of bringing about repentance, reconciliation and restoration. It is a very specific and deliberate process. It needs to be employed systematically. It is composed of four specific steps that are to be followed sequentially without deviating, circumventing or reversing the order of steps.

The goal of each step is to solicit repentance from the offender. If it is rendered at any time during the process, the goal has been achieved and the discipline process ends concurrently. This discipline process is one of the greatest gifts Christ has given His church. But the fact of the matter is that no church can do this process if there is no formal membership in the local assembly. Church membership is mandatory for this process to be efficacious.

For one of the steps in the process is to make the offenders accountable to the local "church" if they refuse to repent. In that third step the offender is expected to "listen" to the accountability "of the church."

Why would anyone heed the exhortation and rebuke of the local church if they are not a member of that church? If there's no formal church membership in such an instance, then the discipline process has no teeth or bite whatsoever. And if that's the case, then all individual accountability goes out the window.

Paul also teaches that church membership is necessary for church discipline to work. In 1 Corinthians 5 he commands the local church at Corinth to "expel" the wicked professing believer who refuses to repent of sin after he has been confronted through due process (verse 13). The word for "expel" refers to formally removing someone from membership—in this instance he is talking specifically about formal church membership (ie., those "inside the church"—5:12).

So it is clearly apparent that church discipline, a process Jesus requires of every local church, cannot take place without a formal church membership.

Why Christians Don't Join the Church

We have considered four very significant reasons Christians should become formal members in a local church. Now, let's take a brief look at why countless Christians the world over don't become members despite the Bible's clear teaching.

Ignorance

One common reason Christians don't join the church is because of ignorance. Some believers just don't understand what the Bible actually teaches about membership. This happens because the truth is often shrouded by 2,000 years of formal and informal man-made religious traditions and conventions.

The human tendency through the ages when it comes to religion is to deviate from God's standard and what He actually says in His Word, and then supplant God's truth on any given issue with man-made rules, regulations and customs. The teaching on church membership has not escaped this perennial vice. If this has been true with you then you can be comforted by Jesus' words when He said, "know the truth and the truth will set you free" (John 8:32). Doing things God's way—the way of truth—is always liberating and attendant with His blessings in your life.

Church background

A second reason people don't join the church may be due to their religious background. There are plenty of churches and denominations out there that formally teach that church membership is not taught in the Bible. I have met many Christians of this persuasion. I have had some wonderful Christian people attend and affiliate in my church who were saved or served for years at such churches that taught there is no such thing as required membership.

They like to say, "God's Church is everywhere, all over the world—He knows who His sheep are. He doesn't need a membership list." That sounds quite spiritual, but it simply is naive and not true, as we have already seen what the Bible says on this issue.

Bad previous experiences

A third reason Christians don't join a local church is because they may have had bad previous experiences. Maybe they were at a church that misused the membership process to manipulate the people. Or maybe they were members at a church where they got burned by the pastor or the church leadership. That happens all too commonly, and that is wrong and it grieves Christ. Such pastors and leadership will have to give an account to God for misuse of power (James 3:1). But someone else's sinful behavior does not negate what God commands and expects in other contexts. God still expects Christians to become committed members despite any previous malfeasance on the part of another church.

A lack of commitment

A fourth reason people don't join the church is because they simply do not want to commit. That's how many people are these days—they don't seem to want to commit to anything, be it the church, marriage, relationships, appointments, a job, whatever. They want to reserve the right to do their own thing at any time on a whim.

It's not uncommon for many Christians to have hit-and-miss church attendance for the sole purpose of maintaining their busy leisure schedule, their highfalutin entertainment plans or their extensive travel calendar. "If I join the church," they fear, "then I can't do my own thing." Well...they are right. Being a part of Christ and His Church is not all about doing our own thing or doing what we want—it's all about doing His thing and what He wants (Matthew 6:33).

Fear of accountability

A fifth reason Christians don't want to join the church is because they don't want to become accountable to anyone. Some people don't want to be told what to do—they don't want to answer to anyone...at least not at church! This kind of independent spirit is pervasive in our culture, for after all—this is America—the place where rugged individualism is a virtue, where personal autonomy is prized, and where people are indoctrinated to have it *their* way. As that "Blue Eyes" guy used to sing..."I did it *my* way."

Becoming a church member means being willing to submit oneself and subject oneself to local church authority. But authority is despised in our culture. We are told not to trust authority. Popular bumper stickers and T-shirts enjoin us to "QUESTION AUTHORITY!" Submission, respect and honor for authority are despised, not esteemed. But God's Word is clear on this issue: "he who rebels against authority is rebelling against what God has instituted, and those who do so will bring judgment on themselves" (Romans 13:2).

Many people don't want to become accountable for how they use their time, treasures and talents. To do so is to become vulnerable or even exposed. This kind of living goes against the grain of secular society. It takes supernatural trust and faith to live that way—faith that only God can provide. But the Bible says, "without faith it is impossible to please God." (Hebrews 11:6).

So if such a reluctant spirit characterizes you, and has kept you from joining a local church, then pray and ask God to soften your heart with His Word and His Holy Spirit. Ask Him to give you the right attitude. And if you pray with sincerity you'll find that in time God will indeed answer that prayer and He will change you. He'll do it because it is His perfect will (1 John 5:14).

Too burdensome

A sixth reason people don't join a church is that the process seems too intimidating at times. Becoming a member at some churches requires jumping through countless hoops, passing theological litmus tests, enduring twelve-week membership classes with inordinate homework assignments, writing out and verbally presenting your testimony, and a host of other frightening and laborious requirements. With such rigorous prerequisites it's understandable why some people loathe the infamous membership process.

But it does not have to be that way. Sometimes, simply asking a few questions of the church leadership can alleviate unfounded fears. In most instances church leaders will graciously walk you through the process step by step, even accomodating special needs or requests you might have to help you through the process. If there is formality to the process, that's OK too. Being formal, thorough and systematic is not unspiritual. God wants the church to do all things with excellence and sobermindedness (1 Corinthians 10:31).

Personal differences

A final reason Christians might not formally join the church is because they may have a difference with the local church they are currently attending. This is a frequent occurance. Some might resist formal membership if they disagree with the statement of faith, or maybe they don't agree with some item in the church constitution or philosophy of the church.

In such instances a believer may need to ask why there are differences. He should ask himself if the disagreements are major doctrinal isssues or secondary issues of preference. Tangential issues of preference should not preclude one from joining a Bible-teaching church. On the other hand, if the differences are over core doctrinal issues, then there is a problem. In any case, you may have to choose one of three options.

Option one is to realize that you are at the wrong church...if they are teaching something basic that is not biblical—heretical views on major doctrines, for instanace. If a church denied Jesus' full deity, His virgin birth, the inerrancy of Scripture, the Trinity, salvation by grace through faith alone, and the like, then it would be best to find another church that taught the truth on basic issues. Don't compromise core biblical convictions. Also, don't try to reform any local church by thinking you can single-handedly overturn a local church's entire leadership, constitution, and history. That would just be plain divisive...and futile.

Option two is to consider the possibility that you might be wrong in what you believe about a particular key doctrine. This means you need to maintain a humble and teachable spirit. Ask what God might be trying to teach you in that situation. Maybe He is trying to teach you that you have bad theology in a particular area. That happens on occasion...to everyone. No one but the Trinity and the Bible has a corner on the truth.

Option three pertains to when someone has a secondary disagreement with the church, but not a major doctrinal dispute. There might be a difference regarding style, philosophy, methodology of ministry, or the personality of a pastor. Maybe a given church has good theology, but the music played and sung is not the style or brand of choice, or the lighting is too modern or archaic, or the attire is too stuffy or casual, etc. In such instances, if the church is an advocate to the basics of preaching, discipling, praying and serving in a godly manner then the mature thing to do would be to set aside your personal preferences and join the church in a committed manner.

The church might not even be doing a great job in any of these areas, but if there is at least a biblical conviction to pursue those things, then consider joining that church. Make that church a better and more biblical church by serving it with all your heart. Quit looking for the perfect church! It's not out there. When you serve in a local church, you are not there serving humans, you are there to serve God and Christ. "Whatever you do, work at it with all your heart, as working for the Lord, not for men, since you know that you will receive an inheritance from the Lord as a reward" (Colossians 3:23-24).

That is the essence of being Christ-like. The Bible says we should "consider others better than" ourselves (Philippians 2:3). Be different and set a rare trend by asking yourself not what your church can do for you, but rather what can you do for your church?

Questions for Review
1. How do Luke 15 and John 10 argue for formal church membership?

_____

_____

_____

_____

2. How does Acts 2:41 support the idea of church membership?

_____

_____

_____

3. What is the Greek word for "numbers" in Acts 2:47 and why is that significant?

_____

_____

_____

4. Explain how 1 Peter 5:14 relates to a definite local church membership.

_____

_____

_____

5. Why does church discipline require church membership?

_____

_____

_____

6. List several common reasons Christians don't join the church:

_____

_____

_____

7. Explain why each of those reasons is not biblical:

_____

_____

_____

8. Are you a member of a local church?

_____

_____

_____

9. If you are a member, tell why you think it is important.

_____

_____

_____

_____

10. If you are not a member of a church, explain why not. What is keeping you from joining a church, and soon?

_____

_____

_____

_____

For further study on *Join!* **see these helpful resources:**
The Handbook of Church Discipline, by Jay Adams
Nine Marks of a Healthy Church, by Mark Dever
The Church, by Ed Hayes
To Be or Not to Be a Member, That is the Question!, by Wayne Mack
Life in the Father's House, by Wayne Mack & David Swavely
The Church in God's Program, by Robert Saucy
Spiritual Disciplines Within the Church, by Donald S. Whitney

4

Serve!

"If a man's gift is...serving, let him serve"
(Romans 12:6-7)

The New Testament uses several images and metaphors to describe what the church of Jesus Christ is like. It is called a temple, a bride, a family, and even an army. But the most dominant and the most unique figure is when Paul describes the church as a "body" or more specifically "the Body of Christ."

When Jesus left earth and ascended into heaven He intended His church to represent Him on the earth until He returns again. He planned to fulfill that mission by having the church function as His collective body before the world. The human body is made up of many members, and so is the church—Christians live all over the world. A body is dynamic, with innumerable interdependent functions. That's what the church is supposed to be like. A body is supposed to live, grow and mature. And that is exactly what Christ wants His church to do.

To ensure the growth, health, and maturity of the church of Christ, God has given "spiritual gifts" to the church as a whole, and to its individual members in particular. God's intention and ideal is that all true Christians use their gifts to serve the church to help bring it into conformity with the image of Jesus Christ, which is the ultimate picture of the spiritual maturity that God intends.

So let's look at some foundational principles in the New Testament about spiritual gifts and how they relate to serving the local church.

Every Christian has a Spiritual Gift

The first important truth to remember is that every Christian has a spiritual gift. The Apostle Paul gives a lengthy explanation regarding the purpose and nature of the spiritual gifts in 1 Corinthians chapters 12-14. In that section he plainly states that, "to each [Christian] the manifestation of the Spirit is given" (12:7). The word "manifestation" refers to the "spiritual gifts" he mentions earlier in this chapter in verse one. So he is saying that every Christian has been given a spiritual gift.

And he says again in 12:11 that the Holy Spirit gives spiritual gifts "to each one." The Apostle Peter says the same thing in his first letter when he reminds Christians that they all have received a spiritual "gift" (4:10). So no Christian is left out—all have received at least one spiritual gift.

In 1 Corinthians 12:1 Paul calls these gifts "spiritual" because he wants to emphasize their supernatural and heavenly nature. The word for spiritual is related to the word for "Spirit" which tells us that the gifts are energized by the awesome power of the Holy Spirit of God. In other words, spiritual gifts are not simply natural human aptitudes and talents. These are supernatural enablements given by the same Holy Spirit who helped create the world out of nothing and who raised Jesus from the dead! There is no greater power in the universe. All Christians, no matter how young or old in the faith, have that same supernatural power resident in them!

When do Christians Receive Their Gifts?

The second thing to remember about spiritual gifts has to do with when Christians get their gift. The Bible makes it clear that every Christian receives a gift, or manifestation from the Spirit, at the moment of salvation—the time when he was born again. In 1 Corinthians 12:13 Paul refers to the moment of conversion to Christ as a time when "we were all baptized by one Spirit into the body." What he is saying is that the moment you became a Christian, the Holy Spirit came to live inside of you and instantly God supernaturally joined you to the rest of the body of Christ—and it was at that time you received your spiritual gift.

The last part of 1 Corinthians 12:13 says at the time of salvation, or what Paul calls spiritual "baptism," "we were all given the one Spirit." In other words, you have the Holy Spirit living inside of you and that reality began the moment you became a Christian. So every Christian has the indwelling Holy Spirit. Those who are not Christians, do not have the Holy Spirit of God living inside of them—that is what Paul says in Romans 8:9. And when the Holy Spirit came to live in you He also imparted His supernatural gift to you as a spiritual birthday present. *lost*

On a related matter, some churches teach that you can lose your spiritual gift. They say if you misuse it, neglect it or let it lie dormant, then God will take your gift away. That simply isn't true. Romans 11:29 emphatically states that "God's gifts and call are irrevocable." "Irrevocable" means "unalterable"—that which cannot be reversed. In other words, God is not fickle or capricious. He does not take back His gifts. He's not double-minded or stingy. He is not going to take your spiritual gift away.

Your spiritual gift is as secure as your eternal salvation. As long as you have the indwelling Holy Spirit living in you, then you will have your gifts at your disposal. And if you are truly born again, then the Holy Spirit will never leave you. That's the very promise of Jesus who said, "Never will I leave you; never will I forsake you" (Hebrews 13:5). Will the Holy Spirit ever leave you? The Bible says unequivocally, "Never!"

How do You Get Your Spiritual Gift?

The third principle has to do with how Christians get their spiritual gifts. Some would have us believe that in order to get a spiritual gift from God we must pray, beg, plead and even cajole God, if necessary. But that is not the case. God will not be manipulated by human will or cunning.

The Bible clearly teaches that God gives the spiritual gifts sovereignly, as He chooses, not as we choose. He created us. He knows us best. He knows how we should best function. He knows best what the church needs for growth and health. He's in charge; He's the boss—not us. And He is the Author and Dispenser of the spiritual gits.

1 Corinthians 12:11 says God gives the spiritual gifts "just as He determines." In 12:18 it says that "God has arranged the parts in the body, every one of them, just as He wanted them to be." In Hebrews 2:4 it says that God the Father confirmed the gospel message by giving "gifts of the Holy Spirit according to His own will." So, at the moment of salvation, a Christian gets a spiritual gift at the discretion of God—"according to His own will"—not ours.

71

This truth is actually very comforting and liberating, for each of us can be assured that we are perfectly gifted by God in accord with how He wants each of us to be used in the body—we don't have to vie for a gift that is not ours out of peer pressure, the fear of man, or just to impress others. Father knows best!

There are Different Gifts

The fourth truth about spiritual gifts is that there are a variety of gifts. Not all Christians have the same gift; they aren't supposed to. That is not God's design. That would not be healthy. Again 1 Corinthians 12 is crystal clear on this, which states, "There are different kinds of gifts" (verse 4). And Romans says the same thing: "We have different gifts, according to the grace given us" (12:6). Peter affirms the same principle as he points out the reality that spiritual gifts vary among the members (1 Peter 4:10-11).

There are many wonderful implications in this truth that there are different spiritual gifts. It tells us that God loves variety—He is a complex, diverse and creative God, and that is reflected in His design of the variegated nature of the church and the multi-faceted bestowal of its gifts.

It also tells us that all the gifts, and therefore all Christians, are important to the church, the Body of Christ. For God wants all Christians, regardless of their gifts, to be contributing to the service and growth of the church by use of their different gifts. Every Christian is vital to the health and maturity of the church. No believer is insignificant or without value.

Having a variety of gifts provides healthy balance and equilibrium in the Body of Christ. Paul asks rhetorically, "what if the whole body were an eye, where would the sense of hearing be?" (1 Corinthians 12:17). That's like asking, "what if a football team had eleven running backs on the field, where would the quarterback be?" Such a notion is absurd, for that would make for one lousy, ineffectual, lop-sided football team. The same with the church. A variety of gifted people with a variety of gifts allows for the kind of balance and healthy growth that God intended.

Spiritual Gifts are Defined by the New Testament

Closely related to the fourth truth above is truth number five which is that the spiritual gifts are clearly delineated in the New Testament. I say the New Testament because we are talking about the spiritual gifts of the "church," the Body of Christ. In the Old Testament there were gifts and gifted people, but in the New Testament God reveals a whole new program, plan, and nature of gifts specifically suited for the New Testament church that did not exist in the Old Covenant.

This is what Paul is talking about in Ephesians when he says that Christ "gave [spiritual] gifts" when He "ascended on high" (Ephesians 4:8). These gifts were not given to the church until after Christ was crucified, died, rose and ascended into heaven. So these are unique gifts. For example, one of the New Testament spiritual gifts is called "apostleship" (1 Corinthians 12:28). Apostles (nor the gift of apostleship) clearly did not exist in the Old Testament. Apostles began to function for the first time with the ministry of Jesus, who hand-picked such candidates for the gift. So we are dealing with a new order of gifts for a new era and new dispensation—the "church age."

Further, these gifts are explicitly called gifts for and of the "body" which is the "church" (1 Corinthians 12). The church did not exist in the Old Testament.

And Paul calls these the gifts of the "Holy Spirit" which means the gifts are imparted and engergized by the indwelling Spirit of God in every believer. The believers in the Old Testament did not all have the indwelling Holy Spirit—that reality is a benefit and result of the New Covenant that did not become a reality until after the resurrection of Christ and the giving of the Holy Spirit at the time of Pentecost when the church was born (Jeremiah 31:33 ff.; Ezekiel 36:26-27; John 7:37-39).

So when people have you take spiritual gift inventories and other tests to try to discern what your gift might be, make sure they are using gifts of the Holy Spirit as delineated in the New Testament. For I have seen some tests where they list the gifts uniquely given to the two obscure guys in Moses' day who were specially called by God to be metallurgists and gem-stone cutters for designing the Old Testament tabernacle and all of its accouterments (Exodus 35:30-35). The problem with that is nowhere in the Bible does it say that their initimable gifts were perpetual, to be replicated, or even designed for the growth of the New Testament church.

The spiritual gifts of the New Testament church are listed primarily in 1 Corinthians 12, Romans 12 and Ephesians 4. These three passages refer to eighteen specific gifts. The eighteen gifts can be categorized into various groupings according to their function. One suggestion is as follows:

A. Gifts of Revelation and Inspiration
    1) the word of knowledge (1 Corinthians 12:8)
    2) the word of wisdom (1 Corinthians 12:8)
    3) apostleship (1 Corinthians 12:28; Ephesians 4:11)
    4) prophecy (1 Corinthians 12:28; Ephesians 4:11)

B. Gifts of Verification and Validation
    5) healing (1 Corinthians 12:9)
    6) miracles/powers (1 Corinthians 12:10)
    7) tongues/languages (1 Corinthians 12:10)
    8) the interpretation of tongues (1 Corinthians 12:10)
    9) discerning of spirits (1 Corinthians 12:10)
    10) faith (1 Corinthians 12:9)

C. Gifts of Perpetuation and Edification
    11) pastor-teachers (Ephesians 4:11)
    12) teacher (1 Corinthians 12:28)
    13) evangelist (Ephesians 4:11)
    14) exhortation/encouragement (Romans 12:8)
    15) ministry/helps/service (Romans 12:7)
    16) giving (Romans 12:8)
    17) showing mercy (Romans 12:8)
    18) administration/governing/leading (Romans 12:8; 1 Cor 12:28)

The first two categories of gifts (A and B) are also called "sign" gifts and were dominant during the founding of the church and among the apostles and New Testament prophets (2 Corinthians 12:12). The gifts of "revelation" and "verification" authenticated and validated the gospel message of the apostles and prophets before the New Testament was written down (Hebrews 2:3-4).

After the New Testament was completed these gifts became obsolete (1 Corinthians 13:8) and the written Scriptures became the standing authority for the New Testament church (Ephesians 2:19-20; 2 Timothy 3:16-17; 2 Peter 3:14-16; Jude 3).

The gifts of "edification" (category C) continue on in perpetuity, as the Holy Spirit energizes the saints to utilize them in ministry. The pastor-teachers, evangelists and teachers have supplanted the role of the apostles and prophets by providing leadership in today's church. Helps, giving, mercy, governing, and exhortation are complementary auxiliary gifts that add the needed balance to the diverse needs of a growing church today.

God Uses Different Gifts at Different Times

The sixth truth is that God employs the use of different spiritual gifts at different points in church history. In other words, all the New Testament spiritual gifts are not in operation simultaneously during the Church era—God does not use all the gifts all at the same time. Some gifts will be in operation while others may not be.

Back to the football team—every football team needs all the different players (gifts), both offense and defense. But you don't play all of the players all at the same time. You don't play the quarterback on defense. The middle linebacker does not play on offense when it's time to score. The different gifts and positions are employed at different times for strategic purposes. That is also true in the church with respect to the spiritual gifts.

The simplest illustration of this often overlooked truth pertains to the gift of apostleship. The New Testament age began with the incarnation of Jesus Christ, and more pointedly, with the commencement of His public ministry. The first New Testament spiritual gift to be introduced was the gift of "apostleship" when Jesus called His twelve apostles (Matthew 10:1-2).

He spent three years training these twelve for the purpose of being deployed later, when the church began forty days after His resurrection (Acts 2). The twelve apostles were eventually to become the first members and the foundation of the church when it began on Pentecost Sunday. The apostles did not begin to formally employ their gift of apostleship until after the church began (Acts 1:4-8). Once the Holy Spirit came to live inside them they began to build the church as they utilized their spiritual gifts with enthusiasm.

As the apostles laid the foundation of the church early on, the gift of "pastor-teacher" had not yet been fully employed. That gift would engage full bore after the apostles finished their work of laying the foundation of the church. The gift of pastor eventually supplanted the gift of apostleship. There are no apostles today, but there are pastors in every church. The first Christian church existed in Jerusalem. The leadership in that church included apostles and the elders, but it makes no reference to "pastors." The gift of apostleship chronologically existed before others and is obsolete today.

So God uses different spiritual gifts at different times in the development and growth of the church. In the early church the "sign" gifts abounded—today, the secondary and service gifts are in operation.

Christians are Commanded to Use Their Gifts

Seventh, Christians are commanded to use or employ their spiritual gifts. First Peter 4:10 says every believer "should use whatever gift he has" by "faithfully administering" it. This is a command for all Christians. And when God gives us a command and we choose to disobey or ignore it, then that is sin. Many people become Christians and then get into the pattern of just "going to church." They go and sit in the pews and listen to the preacher and then leave, never having contributed by using their gifts. This is not God's plan.

God's plan is that all Christians find a place in the local church where they can serve by employing their spiritual gifts for the edification of other individual Christians and for the growth of the Body overall. Paul says in Ephesians 4:16 that God wants "each part [to do] its work." That means every Christian should have a ministry in the church. What is your ministry? Every Christian should be able answer that question.

Going back to 1 Peter 4:10, it says all Christians are supposed to "faithfully" employ their gifts. The word for "faithful" is *oikonomoi* which is where we get our word "economy." It refers to being a good steward. A steward is one entrusted to take care of someone else's valuables and make good use of them until they are returned in the future for a detailed accounting. In other words, we are "stewards" of the spiritual gifts God has given us at salvation and someday He is going to judge and evaluate us on how faithful we were in employing our spiritual gifts in service to the church.

First Corinthians 3 says in the future all our spiritual ministry will be scrutinized and carefully evaluated by the Lord Jesus, and our "work will be shown for what it is, because the Day [of Judgment] will bring it to light. It will be revealed with fire, and the fire will test the quality of each man's work" (v. 13). In other words, at the Judgment Jesus is going to blow-torch all of the work we did on earth, and whatever was of true value, like gold, silver and precious stones, will survive the fire. Whatever was superficial and worthless will be consumed and exposed for being non-efficacious—of no eternal value to the cause of Christ.

It goes on to say, "If what he has built survives, he will receive his reward" (v. 14). This means we will get eternal rewards in heaven for faithfully using our spiritual gifts here on earth. That is a great incentive to use your gifts now.

The passage concludes by saying, "If it is burned up, he will suffer loss; he himself will be saved, but only as one escaping through the flames" (v. 15). Here Paul is saying that if a Christian uses his gift in the wrong way or fails to use it to its potential then there will be a loss of eternal rewards in heaven. You can lose heavenly privileges through poor, lazy stewardship. So don't lose out—start using your spiritual gifts today!

Spiritual Gifts are for Serving Others

Eighth, Spiritual gifts are for serving others. First Corinthians 12:7 says we are to employ our gifts "for the common good." That means we serve to benefit *others* in the church. It's not all about "me."

In 1 Corinthians 14:12 Paul says that Christians should use their gifts to "build up the church." The word for "build up" is a compound word from the Greek *oikos* meaning "house" and *domeo* meaning "to build." It means to "edify" or "to build up another person." This is a selfless act of love. It means God gave us spiritual gifts to benefit others, not ourselves.

The Corinthians royally missed the boat on this point. They were a church abounding in spiritual gifts. When writing them a long letter of rebuke and correction, Paul starts the epistle by acknowledging that they did "not lack any spiritual gift." Their problem was that they were using their gifts in a self-serving manner and for the wrong reasons—to show-boat and be popular. This was creating large-scale division in the church (1:11-12) and tearing the church down (3:3). They were abusing their spiritual gifts.

When Christians use their spiritual gifts to edify themselves and not others, Paul says this is a "worthless" and "childish" endeavor—it accomplishes "nothing" good whatsoever (13:3; 14:20).

This is a pertinent truth for the church today. Christians the world over are seeking the showy, fancy gifts, like speaking in tongues, for the sole purpose of edifying themselves. This is shameful.

Some Christians advocate speaking in tongues privately in a closet, calling it their "private prayer language", for the purpose of self-edification and self-gratification. There are two huge problems with such a notion. First of all, such a practice is the very antithesis of what Paul says should be done. He says pointedly that speaking in tongues should be done only in the presence of others, with an intelligible interpretation rendered every time for the sole purpose of edifying others, not self (14:5-18). Note his strong words: "But in the church I would rather speak five intelligible words to instruct others than ten thousand words in a tongue" (14:19).

The second major flaw is the confusion of speaking in tongues with private prayer. God never intended speaking in tongues to be used as a secret, private prayer language. When the disciples asked Jesus, "Lord, teach us to pray," He did not tell them to "speak in tongues." He could have, but He didn't.

Instead He responded by showing them the one true model of prayer—the *Lord's Prayer* (Luke 11:1-4). It was a blueprint of how believers were to pray in "private" or in "secret", by themselves, as Jesus makes clear in Matthew 6:6. It's a model of prayer using normal, intelligible words—not unintelligible ones like speaking in tongues.

There are literally hundreds of prayers recorded in the Bible by the saints of all the ages, and all those prayers are spoken in everyday, understandable language—not in uninterpreted tongues. Conversley, there are no examples in the Bible of a believer praying privately to God by "speaking in tongues."

Moses' prayer of jubilation at the Exodus (Exodus 15); Joshua's prayer of repentance (Joshua 7); Hannah's prayer of petition (1 Samuel 2);

Solomon's prayer of dedication (1 Kings 8); Job's prayer of humiliation (Job 42); David's prayer of confession (Psalm 51); Daniel's prayer of reflection (Daniel 9); Jesus' prayer of intercession (John 17); and the angelic prayers of adoration (Revelation 5) are examples of the greatest, most effacacious and exemplary prayers in the Bible. And they are all spoken and communicated with normal, intelligible words—not through speaking in tongues.

Love is Greater than the Gifts

Ninth, spiritual gifts are to be employed in the context of love. That is Paul's main argument in 1 Corinthians 12 through 14. Paul discusses the spiritual gifts in chapter 12 and 14, and sandwiched in the middle is a beautiful exposition of love in action (13:1-13).

His point is that the gifts need to be centered on love and they need to flow out of love—and his writing is an apt illustration of the priority of love by having the discussion of gifts positioned like bookends on either side of his discussion of the priority of love.

Paul defines love in 1 Corinthians 13. There he says love is a self-less act of sacrifice with the goal of meeting the needs of others (1 Corinthians 13:1-7). Love is the motive for using the spiritual gifts.

But it is possible to go through the motions of employing the gifts without love. That's what the Corinthians were doing, and they were soundly rebuked by Paul for their charismatic narcissism. He emphatically states, "If I speak in ...tongues...but have not love, I am only a resounding gong or a clanging cymbal" (13:1). In other words, if love is not my motive when using my spiritual gifts in the church, then all my activity is a bunch of meaningless noise that accomplishes nothing.

Paul goes on to say that in the local church, love is a greater priority than the use of any of the gifts, for love is an eternal and permanent virtue, whereas all the gifts are ultimately transitory—they will pass with time after they have served their purpose of helping build the church.

So make a commitment to use your gift of service "in love." Ask God to help you keep your motives pure in all that you do for Him.

Not Every Christian has the Same Gift

Tenth, not every Christian has the same gift. This truth is basic but is widely misunderstood and confused in the church today. There are many pastors and Bible teachers and spiritual gift gurus out there exhorting

Christians to aspire for certain gifts or even all the gifts. A common teaching is the idea that every Christian is expected to speak in tongues. But such a notion is foreign and contrary to true Bible teaching.

For example, Paul clearly says in 1 Corinthians 12 that "not all are apostles; not all are prophets; not all are teachers; not all work miracles; not all have the gift of healing; not all speak with tongues; not all interpret [tongues]" (vv. 29-30).

Literally he is reminding the Corinthians that not every Christian has the gift of apostleship. Not every Christian has the gift of tongues or the interpretation of tongues, etc. Not every Christian has the same gift. Nor does any Christian have all the gifts. God has distributed the gifts among the body as "He wanted them to be" (12:18). Yet, it is not uncommon to hear pastors telling their people that every one of them needs to and should speak in tongues. This is a direct contradiction to what the Bible teaches.

"Apostleship" is one of the spiritual gifts listed in Corinthians, and yet it is clear from Scripture that the office of "apostle" was limited to just a few men in the early church. That gift became obsolete after the foundation of the church was successfully laid down in the first century (Ephesians 2:20).

Further, not every Christian was given the gift of "prophecy"—that gift was for a limited number of people and even for a limited time. Prophets were used by God to help lay the foundation of the church. And then Paul tells us that in time, with the maturing of the early church, that gift would "cease" (1 Corinthians 13:8).

There are no "prophets" today. Prophets received direct revelation from God. Today we have the Bible—it contains all the revelation we need. It is totally sufficient for all faith and Christian practice (Jude 3). Nevertheless, there are plenty of self-proclaimed prophets in churches all over who think they speak for God, thus usurping the authoritative role exclusively reserved in these last days for God's Word, the Bible.

The widespread idea that there are modern day apostles and prophets and that every Christian should be speaking in tongues is actually a modern day phenomenon. These notions were categorically rejected by the Christian church for the first eighteen hundred years after the first century. When such notions did sporadically occur, they were rejected as spurious and unbiblical. Today, unfortunately, in a day when relativism, postmodernism, and political correctness have set the tone in the realm of ideas, this wrong thinking has flourished and permeated the church universal.

The Spiritual Gifts are for the Local Church

Eleventh, the spiritual gifts are to be used by Christians *in* the local church. They are to be employed in the local church for the purpose of building up and growing the church. By "church" we mean all the redeemed people who belong to Christ's family. The Church of Christ is people, not a place.

Jesus made a great promise in Matthew 16:18: "I will build My Church and the gates of Hades will not overcome it." In this verse Jesus predicted He would build His Church. The Church is the only institution in the New Testament that Jesus promised to invest in. Jesus never promised to build a company, an institution of higher learning, a para-church organization, a *Fortune 500* firm, or a great country. Rather He is committed to building His Church.

And He has been building it for nearly 2,000 years. He promised that death itself ("Hades") would not defeat the Church. Jesus is all-powerful and all-knowing. What He purposes to do always comes to pass. So the Church will continue on perpetually, victoriously, with Christ as the Master-Builder.

Wal-Mart, Microsoft, Tiger Woods, the New England Patriots and the United States of America may be super-powers today. But fifty, 100 or 500 hundred years from now they may be just forgotten memories, whereas the Church of Christ will live on, in continuity, as the only eternally significant super-power. Jesus said so.

Don't you want to be part of a winning team? If you are a part of Jesus' Church, you will be a winner. The Church will continue to grow and flourish until it reaches completion. The culmination and coronation day of the Church is assured. D-Day is coming! What Jesus started back on Pentecost Sunday, the birthday of the Church, He will bring to fruition. This is what Paul meant when he said that as Christians all use their gifts of service in the local church it will contribute to the maturation of the Body. And as Christians use their gifts,

The body of Christ may be built up until we all reach unity in the faith and in the knowledge of the Son of God and become mature, attaining to the whole measure of the fullness of Christ (Ephesians 4:12-13).

One amazingly exciting truth about Jesus' promise to build His Church is that He has chosen to build it through *us*—by using saved sinners to be His sub-contractors, foremen, laborers, apprentices and servants. The Bible says, "we are God's fellow workers"! (1 Corinthians 3:9). We get to co-labor with Almighty God as we help build His Church, for He has "assigned to each [Christian] his task" in the building process (3:5). Every Christian has a job to do.

The hit TV show "Extreme Makeover—Homeowners Edition" is growing in popularity. In seven days a work crew of countless dozens of contractors, carpenters, builders, designers and decorators refurbish entire homes that are dilapidated and transform them into exquisite model lots.

The show can be quite inspiring for its philanthropic efficacy toward some very needy families. Those who work for the show often give testimony to the sense of fulfillment and satisfaction they feel after helping others in need by imparting tangible blessings to them. How much more satisfaction and fulfillment the Christian can have who co-labors with God in the process of helping to build the institution of the Church—the Body of Christ—by serving her with spiritual gifts that bestow more than temporal blessings—but rather supernatural and eternal ones.

There will be Rewards in Heaven for Spiritual Service

Finally, Christians who faithfully serve the church in this life with their spiritual gifts will be rewarded by God in the next life. The concept of receiving heavenly rewards from God in the next life is clearly biblical. Although some people reject the notion as crass, "fleshly" and unspiritual, the Bible teaches otherwise. Jesus promised, "I am coming soon! My reward is with me" (Revelation 22:12). First Corinthians 3:14 says every Christian "will receive his reward" on "the Day" Christ returns—and the rewards will correspond to faithful Christian service and ministry in this life.

One of the most misunderstood verses in the Bible is 2 Corinthians 5:10. It says, "For we must all appear before the judgment seat of Christ, that each one may receive what is due him for the things done while in the body, whether good or bad." A cursory reading in the English text may make one think that even Christians will be punished for their sins when they get to Heaven as they are confronted by Jesus the Judge. But nothing could be further from the truth.

If you are a Christian then all of your sins have been forgiven by Christ—past, present and future. That is what Jesus meant when He said while on the cross, "It is finished!" (John 19:30). Romans 8:1 clearly says that for the Christian there "is no condemnation [punishment/ eternal judgment] for those who are in Christ Jesus"! Jesus died on the cross for all of your sins, not just most of them. He was punished so you won't be. That is the gospel—that is the "good news"!

So then what is 2 Corinthians 5 talking about? The actual Greek words used in that verse clarify its true meaning. This judgment throne is called the "bema," as opposed to other places of judgment like the Great White Throne Judgment in Revelation 20. The Great White Throne is where only unbelievers will appear to be condemned by God. Only believers will appear before the "bema"—the Judgment seat of Christ.

At the "bema" judgment believers will be rewarded for "the things done" in terms of Christian service. Faithful ministry will be rewarded and superficial, self-serving religious works will not be rewarded. It's kind of like at the Olympics—the judgment throne is like an awards ceremony for those who are deserving based on their fruitful activity.

The losers in the Olympics are not punished, thrown in jail, fined or given penance for not winning. They simply don't get an award or special recognition. They lose out on the privilege of standing up on that prestigious platform during the national anthem. This has nothing to do with initial salvation—no one can earn or work for their salvation (Ephesians 2:8-9). No sinful human deserves God's forgiveness. This has to do with the works that the Holy Spirit produces in the life of a Christian based on his obedience and faithfulness in ministry.

The empty, fruitless activity done by the Christian is described as "bad." A better translation would be "worthless—having no eternal value or significance." It does not mean "sinful." So the "bema" judgment will not be a place of punishing sins—but of rewarding good works in the life of the Christian.

Related to this truth is the amazing verse of Ephesians 2:10 which says, "For we are God's workmanship, created in Christ Jesus to do good works, which God prepared in advance for us to do." This verse tells us that in eternity past, God planned for us to do certain works of service for Him when we became Christians. That is one of the reasons He created us—to serve Him with good works (after we get saved) that He designated before the universe existed. And He had every Christian in mind—assigning to every one of them very specific tasks to fulfill.

So we are stewards of these "good works" that God has entrusted to us to accomplish. One of the key ways we accomplish these spiritual good works is by employing our spiritual gifts of service. And one day when Jesus returns, He will evaluate whether we dispatched our duty of service. If we have, then we will here these blessed words: "Well done, good and faithful servant! You have been faithful with a few things: I will put you in charge of many things. Come and share your Master's happiness" (Matthew 25:21).

Questions for Review

1. List three key New Testament passages that describe the spiritual gifts (give the book and chapter)

_____

_____

_____

_____

2. How are spiritual gifts different than natural gifts or aptitudes?

_____

_____

_____

_____

3. Who receives a spiritual gift? (give a reference to support your answer)

_____

_____

_____

_____

4. When does a person receive his/her spiritual gift? (give a verse reference to support your answer)

_____

_____

_____

_____

5. Is every Christian supposed to speak in tongues? Why or why not? (give references to support your answer)

_____

_____

_____

_____

6. How are the gifts listed in 1 Corinthians 12 different than the ones mentioned in Ephesians 4 and Romans 12?

_____

_____

_____

_____

7. Is "apostleship" a spiritual gift? Is it a gift that exists today? Why or why not?

_____

_____

_____

_____

8. What is the main purpose of the gifts?

_____

_____

_____

_____

9. What is your spiritual gift and how are you employing it in the local church today?

_____

_____

_____

_____

10. Why is love greater than the spiritual gifts?

_____

_____

_____

_____

For further study on *Serve!* **see these helpful resources:**
19 Gifts of the Spirit, Leslie B. Flynn
Unwrapping Your Spiritual Gifts, by Kenneth Gangel
Speaking in Tongues, Robert Lightner
Speaking in Tongues, Bernard Ramm
Improving Your Serve, by Charles Swindoll
Understanding Spiritual Gifts, by Robert L. Thomas

5

Disciple!

"go and make disciples of all nations..."
(Matthew 28:19)

What is the mission of the church? Depending on who you ask, you'll get a disparity of answers. The most common answer that Christians give goes something like this: "The mission of the church is to evangelize people—to get people saved!" But that is not the mission of the church. That is only one part of Christ's mission or goal for the church. The mission of the church is broader than that—the mission of the church is "to make disciples of all nations"—that's what Jesus said. Since this is our main mission as Christians, we had better be clear as to what it means. To that end let's look at the New Testament teaching on "making disciples."

The Great Commission is Our Mission
Jesus is the Savior, Lord and Head of the Church. He is the One who said 2,000 years ago, "I will build my church" (Matthew 16:18). So He knows what the mission of the church is and He has revealed to believers what that mission is. He gave the mission in Matthew 28 after His resurrection just before He ascended into heaven. On the mountain in Galilee Jesus said this to His eleven disciples:

> *All authority in heaven and on earth has been given to me. Therefore go and make disciples of all nations, baptizing them in the name of the Father and of the Son and of the Holy Spirit, and teaching them to obey everything I have commanded you (Matthew 28:18-20).*

This command of Jesus has come to be known as "The Great Commission" for the church. This passage, more than any other, distills and crystallizes the focus of the church. What are Christians supposed to be doing while here on earth? Why did Jesus put us here? How shall believers occupy their time, coordinate their efforts and invest their resources until Jesus returns? The answer is here, in the Great Commission. The church is here to "make disciples."

Make the Main Thing the Main Thing

As you read Matthew 28:18-20, what do you think the main thing is or the main command in the passage? Relying solely on your English translation can be confusing and even misleading. The popular translations can make it appear that "go," "baptizing," and "teaching" are the main verbs or main commands in the passage. But they are not! The main verb is "make disciples." In the Greek text this phrase is actually just one word, which is a verb, and it is a command—the word is *matheteuo*.

Matheteuo means "to instruct, to train, to discipline." In its verb form it can be translated "to disciple" or just "disciple." The words "go," "baptizing," and "teaching" in this passage are all participles and they all modify the main verb, *matheteuo*. The three participles tell us how we are supposed to "make disciples." So in the words of Jesus, the main thing for the church to be doing is to be "discipling" others by means of "going," "baptizing," and "teaching."

Going

The first step in discipling is "going." This refers to the job Christians have as "ambassadors" (2 Corinthians 5:20). Believers are supposed to go out into the world, infiltrating it to the uttermost parts, and boldly proclaim the gospel of Jesus Christ, living in a godly way to make the message believable. Refer to the chapter on Go! to see how this is accomplished.

Baptizing

After "going" and sharing the gospel, inevitably some people will respond to the good news by believing and committing to it. People will get saved. When that happens, we employ step two of the discipling process which entails "baptizing." This is when we help new believers formally assimilate into the local church through membership, support and basic orientation. They are now identifiable members of the church family. For more details on this aspect of discipling, see the chapter on *Join!*

Teaching

The third and final step of the discipling process is "teaching." This is the life-long process of helping new believers grow in their faith so they can mature and become spiritually healthy and fruitful for Christ. This aspect of discipling is the emphasis of this chapter.

Jesus was the Master Disciple-Maker

If we want to disciple the right way then we better imitate Jesus. The Apostle Paul said. "Follow my example, as I follow the example of Christ" (1 Corinthians 11:1). So Jesus is the exemplar.

Jesus spent more than three years making disciples. Those who followed Him were called "disciples." "Disciple" means "a follower, a learner." The word "disciple" is used more than 250 times in the Gospels and Acts. The simplest definition of what Jesus meant by "disciple" or "discipleship" is in Matthew 4:19, where Jesus said, "Come follow me...and I will make you fishers of men." A disciple is a follower of Christ.

The word "disciple" is frequently confused with the word "apostle." The two words are not synonymous. "Apostle" means "a sent one," like a formal representative of another—an "ambassador." In the Gospels the word "apostle" was reserved for the twelve select men that Jesus chose to begin His church upon His departure.

"Disciple" is a more general term and simply means "student" or "follower." The twelve apostles were "disciples" of Jesus; but not every disciple of Jesus was an "apostle." Notice the distinction Luke makes between the two groups when he writes, "One of those days Jesus went out to a mountainside to pray, and spent the night praying to God. When morning came, he called his *disciples* to him and chose twelve of them, whom he also designated *apostles*" (6:12-13).

Jesus was very deliberate and strategic as He discipled. His whole ministry was one of discipleship. We can learn from His example. The way He discipled can be generally divided into two categories: 1) macro-discipleship and 2) micro-discipleship.

Macro-discipleship

Macro-discipleship was when Jesus taught, trained, instructed and ministered to large groups. An example would be the Sermon on the Mount where Jesus preached to "the crowds" (Matthew 5:1). This could have been hundreds or even thousands of people at one time. Another example of Jesus' macro-discipleship is when He ministered to a "large crowd" by teaching, healing and feeding them. Matthew says there were more than 5,000 people in attendance that day (Matthew 14:13-21).

Macro-discipleship, or corporate discipleship, was a central part of Jesus' ministry. Spiritual ministry to large crowds is essential for inculcating a group worldview and consciousness that builds unity. Large group discipling is essential to the health and the growth of the body as a whole. The church needs to remember this very important component of Jesus' ministry. It cannot be neglected or marginalized for other methods.

Unfortunately that is happening today in the church. In their zeal for the benefits that attend small-group dynamics, some churches are abandoning large-group ministry altogether and focusing solely on small "cell-groups" as the one true spiritual panacea that supposedly will reinstate true early New Testament ministry. But this approach lacks balance and is not true to the New Testament, the nature of Jesus' ministry, or to the early church dynamic.

The New Testament, Jesus, and the early church all incorporated macro-discipleship—or "large group" ministry—as a vital and essential element to Christian growth and development. In examining the four Gospels, it is apparent that Jesus spent nearly twenty percent of His teaching time with large groups. The early church gathered together regularly in large groups for formal times of worship and fellowship—crowds as large as 120 (Acts 1:15), 3,000 (Acts 2:41), 5,000 and more (Acts 4:4). "All the believers were together" for corporate worship on a regular basis (Acts 2:42-47). Paul said that the believers "come together as a church" to practice the ordinances as a group (1 Corinthians 11:18). That is macro-discipleship. And the New Testament commands the church to continue the legacy of regular macro-discipleship, or corporate fellowship, to help with the edification process (Hebrews 10:24-25).

Micro-discipleship

In addition to macro-discipleship, Jesus practiced micro-discipleship. This was concentrated discipleship to smaller groups of people, including one-on-one discipling. According to the four Gospels, Jesus spent an amazing thirty-two percent of His time ministering to or discipling individuals. He spent twenty-three percent of His time with one or more of His twelve apostles alone. From the data, it is evident that Jesus struck a beautiful balance with respect to how He spent His time discipling—He valued large group ministry, small group ministry, and one-on-one ministry. This model needs to drive our discipling methodology.

A closer look at the Gospels reveals that Jesus put a premium on micro-discipleship. The Gospel of John shows Jesus ministering to the crowds for the first twelve chapters. And then a transition takes place. From chapter thirteen on He has a privatized ministry to only the twelve apostles and other select disciples. With the crowds Jesus could emphasize the breadth of His ministry, but with the small groups and individuals He could concentrate on the intimate depth of His ministry through personalized discipling. The rest of this chapter will highlight the means and the methods of micro-discipleship modeled by Jesus and His apostles.

There is a Goal in Discipling

The stated purpose in the discipling process is clear: Jesus said, "A student is not above his teacher, but everyone who is fully trained will be like his teacher" (Luke 6:40). The word for "student" here is *mathetes*, the noun for our earlier verb *matheteo*—"to disciple." So the goal of discipling is to bring a convert and follower of Jesus to full maturity, who will then have the traits and habits of a "teacher" or spiritual "mentor."

Jesus did this very thing with His apostles. He personally selected twelve men who were not spiritually refined. He asked them to follow Him, and for three years He spent quality time with them, living with them, pouring His life into theirs. He taught them, ate with them—laughed and cried with them. He took them everywhere He went. And He modeled godly living before their eyes with the goal of transforming them into His likeness.

With the exception of Judas (whom Jesus knew beforehand would betray Him and fall away as the Old Testament predicted; see John 6:70-71)

Jesus was successful. He trained the eleven disciples to be like Himself. They became the leaders and foundation of the early church (Ephesians 2:19-20). They served Christ faithfully, fully discharging their mission in the face of death. The New Testament gives specific examples of what a "fully trained" disciple looks like. Let's consider the main characteristics.

A mature disciple is Christ-centered

A mature Christian disciple has the right priorities, the first of which is making Christ the center of life. Jesus had high demands for His disciples:

> Large crowds were traveling with Jesus, and turning to them he said: "If anyone comes to me and does not hate his father and mother, his wife and children, his brothers and sisters—yes, even his own life—he cannot be my disciple. And anyone who does not carry his cross and follow me cannot be my disciple" (Luke 14:25-27).

These are strong, and even offensive words from the Lord. But He was speaking parabolically to emphasize that a true disciple will put allegiance to Christ before all other relationships and desires.

A mature disciple is Word-centered

A mature Christian disciple is committed to Jesus' words and teaching which are given in the New Testament:

> To the Jews who had believed him, Jesus said, "If you hold to my teaching, you are really my disciples. Then you will know the truth, and the truth will set you free" (John 8:31-32).

You can't grow spiritually without the truth of the Bible saturating your life. A mature disciple will filter everything through the grid of the Bible, God's Word. A mature disciple will also believe the whole Bible, not just pick and choose as to what suits him. He believes the truth, the whole truth, and nothing but the truth.

A mature disciple preserves unity

Another mark of mature Christian discipleship according to Jesus is the preservation of unity among believers. Jesus said,

> A new command I give you: Love one another. As I loved you, so you must love one another. By this all men will know that you are my disciples, if you love one another (John 13:34-35).

A mature disciple will love other Christians. A divisive, abrasive, chronically critical Christian is immature and "fleshly." That was the Corinthian Christians' problem—Paul said they were sinful for being divisive and hyper-critical (1 Corinthians 1:10-11; 3:3).

A mature disciple bears fruit

Jesus said a mature Christian will be known by his fruits:

> If you remain in me and my words remain in you, ask whatever you wish, and it will be given to you. This is to my Father's glory, that you bear much fruit, showing yourselves to be my disciples (John 15:7-8).

Jesus expected His disciples to "bear fruit," or to produce good works in daily living. Christians should produce action fruit (Matthew 7:15-23) and attitude fruit (Galatians 5:22-23). A disciple of Jesus who does not bear good fruits or good works is a living contradiction. God saved us and put the Holy Spirit inside of us to ensure that we would produce good works. This was God's plan for believers before the world began. Paul tells us in Ephesians that, "we are God's workmanship, created in Christ Jesus to do good works, which God prepared in advance ['*before the world began*'] for us to do" (2:10).

How did Jesus Make Disciples?

Jesus was the Master at making disciples and He commanded His followers to do the same. What would Jesus do about making disciples? The Gospels clearly tell us His strategy. Let's consider some of His disciple-making priorities.

Prayerful selection

As Jesus began His public ministry, word about Him spread quickly and soon multitudes came from far and wide to see Him (Mark 3:8). Throngs of people were fascinated with His unique teaching and deeds (Mark 6:2). Mark 2:13 says a "large crowd came to him." Everywhere He went "many followed him" (Mark 2:15). When Jesus fed the multitudes with just five loaves of bread and two fish in Bethsaida, there were likely more than ten thousand people in attendance (Matthew 14:15-21; Luke 9:10-17). He quickly accumulated many followers.

But Jesus was not impressed with numbers. He would not let human popularity dictate His agenda, nor would He compromise the truth in the face of popular opinion. As a matter of fact, He did not trust the spontaneous flurry of popular sentiment from the multitudes who gave Him high approval ratings. He knew the allegiance of the fickle mob could change like the wind.

> *Now while he was in Jerusalem at the Passover Feast, many people saw the miraculous signs he was doing and believed in his name. But Jesus would not entrust himself to them, for he knew all men. He did not need man's testimony about man, for he knew what was in a man (John 2:23-25).*

This brings us to Jesus' first principle of personal discipleship which is *prayerful selection*. When it came time to disciple a few people in an intimate and intensive manner, Jesus did not hastily gravitate to the many who first showed superficial enthusiasm. Instead, before He committed Himself to investing three years of His life in a select few, Luke 6:12-13 records the following:

> *One of those days Jesus went out to a mountainside to pray, and spent the night praying to God. When morning came, he called his disciples to him and chose twelve....*

Jesus had hundreds of people who were following Him at that time. But He was selective, discriminating and discerning about the few He was going to disciple. And even though He was incarnate Deity, before He decided whom to select He spent the whole night in prayer seeking wisdom from the Father as to who the few should be.

Like Jesus, we need to be fervently prayerful and cautiously selective about whom we are going to disciple on a micro level. We have limited time and resources and we need to be good stewards in decision-making. Being like Jesus includes being prayerful and selective.

Personal association

Making disciples is not merely a formal exercise of regimented meetings to discuss theoretical and esoteric concepts. True discipleship happens first and foremost in the context of personal relationship and friendship. When Jesus chose the twelve men to be His personal disciples, He selected them so that they might "be with him" (Mark 3:14).

Jesus knew that the best way to teach someone, to train them, to influence them, to impact them at the deepest level—was to spend time with them. For three years His disciples went everywhere with Him. Jesus knew the world was His classroom. He was going to maximize His teaching in the venue of everyday living, interpreting the vicissitudes of life for His disciples as they lived day to day.

Jesus called His disciples "friends" (John 15:15). As a true friend, Jesus was transparent, honest, faithful, sacrificial, selfless, loyal and loving. Cultivating a true friendship with a prospective disciple allows one to nurture a quality and depth in spiritual maturity that otherwise could not be achieved in an impersonal, formal, and guarded relationship.

Because Jesus had a personal relationship with His twelve disciples, it afforded Him unique opportunities to train them. His teaching opportunities were not constrained to a classroom for one hour every other week. He was able to teach them everywhere they went—at a wedding (John 2), on the sea (John 6), over meals (John 13), in private, in public (Matthew 11), in homes (John 12), in a garden (Luke 22), at the temple (Matthew 24), on a mountain (Matthew 5).

If we are going to disciple like Jesus, then we need to commit ourselves to cultivating quality personal relationships with those we are discipling. This includes spending quality time together in various contexts of daily living, and a mutual trust of give and take interaction.

Purposeful instruction

In addition to *prayerful selection* and *personal association*, Jesus made a priority of *purposeful instruction* in disciple-making. In the Great

Commission Jesus commanded believers to make disciples by "teaching them to obey everything I have commanded you" (Matthew 28:20).

The word for "teaching" here is *didaskontes*, from which we get our English word "didactics." Didactics has to do with the science of formal teaching and instruction. This word is used in the Gospels forty-seven times, mostly in reference to Jesus' ministry. It consistently connotes Jesus' teaching and preaching of spiritual truths in a systematic, authoritative and purposeful manner.

The main emphasis in what Jesus taught included God, the coming kingdom, righteous living, and salvation. These are the same priorities we need to be teaching as we disciple others. Discipleship is not getting together solely for a good time, or to hang out, or just to talk without specific spiritual objectives orbiting around biblical truth. If there is no mutual learning of biblical truth, then there is no real discipleship taking place.

I thank God for Phil who came into my life when I was saved my freshman year in college. Phil was a junior and was praying for my salvation for the first two months of my college tenure. And as soon as I got saved, Phil tactfully zeroed in on me and began personally discipling me.

Before I knew it we were meeting once a week for prayer, accountability and purposeful instruction. Phil taught me the basic doctrines of the Christian faith. He also introduced me to the discipline of Scripture memorization. We spent an entire semester memorizing 2 Timothy together.

Phil and I also spent time together in other venues in life—we played basketball together, we sang to his guitar in his dorm room, he introduced me to other Christians, we went sight-seeing in downtown Santa Barbara, we watched *March Madness* together. And wherever we went, whatever we did, Phil would filter all of life's circumstances through the grid of Jesus' life and what the Bible had to say on any given issue. Phil understood Jesus' principle of *purposeful instruction.*

When Jesus said we make disciples by "teaching," He had specific content in mind. There is a finite body of doctrine that the Christian is supposed to learn in the discipleship process. That content is defined by Jesus as being "everything [He] commanded" (Matthew 28:20). Everything Jesus commanded specifically refers to the revelation written down by the apostles contained in the New Testament. So in the discipleship-relationship, the discipler needs to make a priority of teaching the disciple major New Testament truths or doctrines.

True spiritual growth and development is contingent upon learning biblical truth. Jesus said, "know the truth, and the truth shall set you free" (John 8:32). Peter said, "Like newborn babies, crave pure spiritual milk, so that by it you may grow up in your salvation" (1 Peter 2:2). The "milk" Peter is referring to is "spiritual milk" which is biblical truth. A Christian cannot grow apart from the regular intake of spiritual nutrients derived from biblical truth and New Testament doctrine.

There are some basic biblical truths that every Christian should master in order to be grounded in the faith. Below is a base-line to include in your own personal discipleship relationships. A key truth is given and supporting Scriptures are given as references.

It would be helpful and even recommended to make a goal of memorizing all the key Scriptures for each truth. Memorizing Scripture is a basic Christian discipline that every believer should cultivate. It's commended and commanded by God many times. For example, God commanded Joshua, "Do not let this Book of the Law depart from your mouth; meditate on it day and night, so that you may be careful to do everything written in it" (1:8). In other words, God was telling Joshua, "Memorize your Bible verses!"

The following are standard verses that will help you all the days of your Christian life, so it is worth the hard work and sweat to commit them to memory:

1. There is only one God
   - ☐ Deuteronomy 6:4
2. Jesus is Deity and equal to God the Father
   - ☐ John 1:1-3
   - ☐ John 1:14
   - ☐ John 8:58
   - ☐ John 17:5
3. God is three distinct Persons
   - ☐ Ephesians 4:4-6
   - ☐ John 14:26
   - ☐ John 16:13
4. The Holy Spirit lives in every Christian
   - ☐ John 14:17
   - ☐ Romans 8:9

5. Jesus is the only way to heaven
   - ☐ John 14:6
   - ☐ 1 Timothy 2:5
6. Salvation is God's gift, not from human works
   - ☐ John 3:16
   - ☐ Ephesians 2:8-9
   - ☐ Titus 3:4-7
   - ☐ 2 Peter 3:9
7. Salvation comes from believing the good news of the Gospel
   - ☐ Acts 16:31
   - ☐ 1 Corinthians 15:1-5
   - ☐ Romans 1:16
   - ☐ Romans 6:23
   - ☐ Romans 10:9-10
8. The Bible is God's Word
   - ☐ 2 Timothy 3:16
   - ☐ Hebrews 4:12
   - ☐ Revelation 22:18-19
9. Christians are expected to be obedient
   - ☐ Ephesians 5:18
   - ☐ Galatians 5:22-23
   - ☐ 1 Thessalonians 5:16-18
10. Every Christian should be a disciple
    - ☐ Luke 9:23-24
    - ☐ John 15:8
    - ☐ 2 Timothy 2:2
11. Every Christian should pray
    - ☐ Philippians 4:6
12. Every Christian will experience suffering
    - ☐ Philippians 1:29
13. The Devil is real
    - ☐ 2 Corinthians 4:4
    - ☐ 1 Peter 5:8
14. Hell is a real place
    - ☐ Matthew 10:28
15. Jesus is coming again
    - ☐ Philippians 3:20-21
    - ☐ 1 Thessalonians 4:16-17

Every Christian is a Disciple

Jesus made it clear that every believer is expected to be a part of the Great Commission. The imperative in the Great Commission, as we have seen, is "to make disciples" (Matthew 28:18-20). So every Christian is involved at some point in the disciple-making process, and as a result every Christian is a disciple—or a learner and follower of Jesus.

Unfortunately some have confused this simple truth. There are Bible teachers who have long propagated the notion that not every believer is a disciple. Rather, they would say that there are two distinct classes of Christians, namely 1) spiritual Christians and 2) non-spiritual or "carnal" Christians. They aver that the spiritual Christians live on a higher plane of commitment than other Christians. These supposed super-saints were catapulted up to the plane of higher living at some "crisis" point that came later in their Christian life. They say the non-spiritual, 'ho-hum' Christians have not had this mystical, empowering crisis experience yet—and they may never have it in this life.

These Bible teachers go on to conclude that only "spiritual" Christians are disciples; "carnal" Christians are not disciples. But in reality this teaching is dead wrong. The New Testament makes no such dichotomy between disciples and Christians nor with spiritual vs. carnal Christians.

The fact is that every Christian is a disciple. Every true believer obtained salvation through the Great Commission, the heart of which is "disciple-making." Every born-again saint enters the kingdom of Christ in this life as a disciple and continues to grow as a disciple through the sanctification process. So discipleship, and all the teaching that Jesus had to say on it in the Gospels, applies to every Christian.

Who's discipling you?

Every Christian should be able to answer two important questions. The first one is, "Who's discipling you?" Every believer should be in a one-on-one discipleship relationship, for a given period of time, with the purpose of achieving clearly defined biblical objectives for personal spiritual growth. Basics should include moral accountability, prayer, study and memorization of Scripture, fellowship and encouragement for one another.

The apostle Paul understood this mandate and single-handedly discipled numerous individuals during the course of his ministry. The best known disciple of his was Timothy (1 Timothy 1:2). And in his letter to Timothy Paul articulated one of the most poignant mandates on biblical discipleship found anywhere in the Bible. He wrote,

> *You then, my son, be strong in the grace that is in Christ Jesus. And the things you have heard me say in the presence of many witnesses entrust to reliable men who will also be qualified to teach others (2 Timothy 2:1-2).*

Some amazing insights about micro-discipleship surface from this short passage. One is that biblical discipleship is a dynamic endeavor that occurs person-to-person. You can't be discipled without getting involved in someone's life—and you have to let that person into your life. Christians who isolate themselves from others and keep people at arm's distance fall prey to a host of subtle temptations.

Another principle from this passage is that true discipleship has the goal of spiritual reproduction. The goal of discipleship is not simply to make another disciple. Rather, the goal of discipleship is to make another disciple-maker! There's a huge difference. The first objective is one-dimensional, short-sighted, parochial and terminal. The latter objective is multi-dimensional, generational, prolific and exponential.

Carefully consider the number of generations that Paul refers to in this discipleship scenario. He begins with himself—the first generation, "the things you have heard from *me.*" He then refers to the second generation disciple, which is Timothy, "the things *you* have heard." Then he tells Timothy to disciple a third generation he calls "*reliable men.*" He concludes with a fourth generation, the spiritual grandchildren of Timothy—those discipled by the third generation—whom he calls "*others.*"

So whoever you are, Christian, plug into the discipleship network by getting under the wing of an older Christian who can help you grow so that you become a disciple-maker, spiritually replicating yourself.

Whom are you discipling?

Speaking of replicating yourself, that leads to the second key question that every Christian should be able to answer with specificity:

"Who are you discipling?" If you are a Christian, then you are a disciple, and if you are a believer you are responsible to fulfill the Great Commission. And the command of the Great Commission is "to make disciples." Who are you discipling?

Some Christians will use the excuse that they don't know enough to disciple anyone. Baloney! Find someone who knows less than you and teach him something. There are no excuses. God knows where we all are on the discipleship continuum, and we all have a part to play and resources to contribute. If you are a parent, your children are your disciples full-time for now. Take that job seriously. If you are a woman, seek women to work with (Titus 2). Consider your walk in life and seek God's will accordingly.

If this is a struggle for you, then begin praying very specifically and regularly the following: "Dear God, thank you for making me a disciple through salvation in Christ. Bring someone into my life to disciple me to help me grow. And give me someone to disciple so I can contribute to the perpetuation of his spiritual journey. In Jesus' name. Amen."

If you keep praying sincerely like that, God will answer your prayer.

Questions for Review

1. What is the mission of the church?

_____

_____

_____

2. What is the "Great Commission" and where is it found in Scripture?

_____

_____

_____

3. What are the three participles in the 'Great Commission' and what is their significance?

_____

_____

_____

_____

4. What is the Greek word for "to make disciples" and what does it mean?

_____

_____

_____

_____

5. What is the difference between a "disciple" and an "apostle"?

_____

_____

_____

6. What is the difference between 'macro-discipleship' and 'micro-discipleship'?

_____

_____

_____

7. What is the goal of discipling?

_____

_____

_____

8. Name three priorities Jesus had in personal discipleship

_____

_____

_____

9. Who are you discipling?

_____

_____

_____

10. Who is discipling you?

_____

_____

_____

For further study on *Disciple!* **see these helpful resources:**

The Adventure of Discipling Others, by Ron Bennett & John Purvis
Christ's Call to Discipleship, by James Montgomery Boice
The Master Plan of Discipleship, by Robert E. Coleman
The Lost Art of Disciple Making, by Leroy Eims
God's Glorious Church, by Tony Evans
Discipleship: Helping Other Christians Grow, by Allen Hadidian
As Iron Sharpens Iron, by Howard Hendricks
The Disciple-Making Church, by Bill Hull
Spiritual Discipleship, by J. Oswald Sanders
Following Christ, by Joseph Stowell
Born to Reproduce, by Dawson Trotman

6

Give!

"the Lord Jesus Himself said:
'It is more blessed to give than to receive' "
(Acts 20:35)

Giving is a Command

God has commanded the church, and Christians in particular, to give. Jesus said, "Give" (Luke 6:38). Paul commanded Christians to give financially to the church (1 Corinthians 16:1-4; Romans 12:8, 13). John exhorted believers to give to those in need (1 John 3:16-18). Hebrews 13:16 says God is pleased when we give to others.

Giving is a basic Christian virtue. Giving to God and others reflects the very nature of God. God's greatest act of loving sacrifice entailed an act of "giving"—"for God so loved the world that He *gave*" (John 3:16). One of the most telling barometers of a person's spiritual maturity is their quotient for giving. God has repeatedly commanded Christians to be giving people, for they are recipients of the greatest gift ever given—salvation in Christ.

This chapter delineates basic biblical principles of giving. God wants us to be gracious givers. And He has enabled us to fulfill that command with discerning priorities in a way that honors Him and blesses others.

God Owns Everything

God owns everything. After all, the Bible says, "God created the heavens and the earth" (Genesis 1:1). He made it all, so He owns it all.

105

David said, "everything in heaven and earth is" God's (1 Chronicles 29:11). Psalm 50:10 declares, "for every animal of the forest is mine, and the cattle on a thousand hills." So every created thing is God's possession, from the cattle on every hill, to every hill with or without cattle. The whole world is God's footstool (Isaiah 66:1).

Because God owns everything, He needs nothing from us. He is totally self-sufficient, independent and autonomous. He is contingent upon nothing. He exists totally apart from us; He is in no way helpless (Acts 17:24-25).

Christians need to be reminded of this truth over and over. How many appeals for money have been made by various religious leaders based on the plea that "God needs your money! You need to tithe now so God can do His work. The enterprise of the church will not go on without your offering"? But the fact of the matter is that God does not need our money. He owns everything! The work of the church will go on whether Christians are stingy and tight-fisted or not. Jesus promised that He would build the church and the gates of hell would not overcome it (Matthew 16:18). That means that nothing, not even human greediness or lack of financial support, will thwart the progress and success of Christ's Church.

Further, because God owns everything, it means that everything we have comes from Him. He is the Divine Dispenser of all good things. Everything we have, everything we own, every blessing that ever came our way came from the sovereign, gracious hand of God the Creator. James 1:17 puts it this way: "Every good and perfect gift is from above, coming down from the Father of the heavenly lights." Your nice car, your children, your spouse, your money, your investments, your talents, your high IQ, your German shepherd, your amiable personality, your house, your job—everything good came from God as a gift.

Paul asks the Christian in 1 Corinthians 4:7, "What do you have that you did not receive?" It's a rhetorical question. He is simply reminding us that everything we have or possess was given to us as a gift. In other words, we did not earn or deserve anything in the ultimate sense. Anything we do have is God's—we are merely stewards of His property.

If we believe that God owns everything, and that we are just momentary stewards on His behalf, then it will be easier for us to share our riches with others. This was the mindset of the early church. Note the following:

> *All the believers were one in heart and mind. No one claimed that any of his possessions was his own, but they shared everything they had. With great power the apostles continued to testify to the resurrection of the Lord Jesus, and much grace was upon them all. There were no needy persons among them. For from time to time those who owned lands or houses sold them, brought the money from the sales and put it at the apostles' feet, and it was distributed to anyone as he had need (Acts 4:32-35).*

They shared EVERYTHING they had! If the church of Christ would only do that today, we'd see great things happen like they did in the early church. Today in America we make money, not just to pay the bills, but also to spend on ourselves first and foremost—for that expensive vacation, those multitudinous, superfluous luxuries, trinkets and toys. Entertainment has become a significant and permanent household line-item in our personal budgets.

Making money in order to share with someone else in need is usually an unplanned after-thought of an occasional happenstance. But that should not be the norm for the Christian. God's design and intent for us is different. For us, one of the main goals of making money should include sharing with others. God commanded Christians to "work, doing something useful with his own hands, that he may have something to *share* with those in need" (Ephesians 4:28).

God Gives the Power to Make Wealth

In Deuteronomy 8:18 God reminded Moses and the Israelites of a profound truth as they were preparing to enter the Promised Land, a land flowing with milk and honey. God told Moses, "But remember the LORD your God, for it is he who gives you the ability to produce wealth." Every penny we make is a result of God's gracious decree of allowing it to happen.

Ultimately, we don't make money because of our slick entrepreneurial dealings, or our creative business acumen, or our mastery over the ebb and flow of the stock market, or because of our fortuitous inheritance passed down to us from wealthy relatives. According to the Bible, any income we have or produce happens because God graciously and sovereignly puts us in a position to make that income. 1 Samuel 2:7 poignantly declares that "the LORD sends poverty and wealth." If you make good money as a medical doctor, then it was God who providentially put you in strategic positions to attain the proper education, training, aptitude and placement to succeed in that field.

A rich professional athlete did not rise to the level of excellence and prominence without God's enablement in every way. God gave Michael Jordan the physical ability and talents to excel. God gave him the drive to work hard and the opportunities to develop his talents. God paved the way for his college scholarship at North Carolina. God helped him land his first NBA contract with the Chicago Bulls. God graciously prevented MJ from ever getting an injury that could have prematurely ended his career. God enables us to make wealth.

The amazing thing about this truth is that it applies to everyone, believers and unbelievers alike. Jesus said God blesses "the evil and the good, and sends rain on the righteous and the unrighteous" (Matthew 5:45). The ability to make money is a gift from God, whether you acknowledge that or not. God reminded the Israelites to always be cognizant of this truth:

> *When you have eaten and are satisfied, praise the LORD your God for the good land he has given you. Be careful that you do not forget the LORD....Otherwise, when you eat and are satisfied, when you build fine houses and settle down, and when your herds and flocks grow large and your silver and gold increase and all you have is multiplied, then your heart will become proud and you will forget the LORD your God...You may say to yourself, "My power and the strength of my hands have produced this wealth for me" (Deuteronomy 8:10-17).*

This is the big lie of modern-day America—"Anyone can achieve the American Dream if he just grits his teeth, works hard, and exercises rugged individualism—he can become financially secure through his own 'power and strength'." It's the American way...the land of opportunity.

But the truth is, it does not always work out that way. The fact is no one gains financial success apart from God's help. He gives the power to make wealth. And we need to always thank Him for it.

Give Regularly

A key principle often neglected by Christians is the command to give regularly. God has commanded Christians to give to the church in a consistent, ongoing and routine manner. All too often, Christians give inconsistently, haphazardly, and lackadaisically. That is not the biblical model.

God is a God of order (1 Corinthians 14:33, 40) and He has prescribed an orderly manner in which Christians are to give. Paul outlines this model of regularity in giving 1 Corinthians 16. He writes,

> *Now about the collection of God's people: Do what I told the Galatian churches to do. On the first day of every week, each of you should set aside a sum of money in keeping with his income, saving it up, so that when I come no collections will have to be made. Then, when I arrive, I will give letters of introduction to the men you approve and send them with your gift to Jerusalem (vv. 1-3).*

Here Paul set a precedent for Christians to set aside money on Sunday—the "first day of every week"—for the purpose of giving it to the church. That is regularity.

Paul also tells the Corinthians to do what the Galatian churches were doing. In other words, the imperative of giving regularly, on the Lord's Day, was not an isolated, localized command given to only one church. It was a universal command Paul wanted implemented in all the churches. And Paul was not giving a casual suggestion here. He was speaking as an authoritative Apostle of Christ and His Church (1 Corinthians 1:1). He was establishing timeless, universal church practice and policy.

Further, in the above passage Paul says to set aside some money to give "in keeping with your income." In other words, as often as you bring in income, from your income you should set some aside to give to

God on the Lord's Day. Today, most people don't get paid as frequently as people did in Paul's day. In New Testament times it was not uncommon to get paid daily or weekly (Matthew 20:1-9). So it was easy to set aside money for every Lord's Day.

Today, many people get paid bi-monthly or even once a month. Or if you work on commission, you might get paid at even more widespread intervals. If that is the case, you can still set aside money to give on the Lord's Day. It's just a matter of planning and prioritizing. It's a matter of being orderly and taking your obligation to give to your local church seriously. You have to pay your bills regularly even though your income may be sporadic or irregular. So you can give to God regularly and consistently if you plan accordingly. If you do, God will bless your faithfulness (1 Samuel 2:30).

There is practical wisdom to giving to the church weekly. The church has bills to pay regularly. Needs arise daily. We need to help sustain the excellence of ongoing ministry. Giving regularly, or weekly, meets that need. Also, God wants us to give regularly because He wants us to have to think about and pray through our financial choices regularly. Money is a daily part of our lives and what we do with every penny needs to be filtered through conscientious deliberation with God, who gave us everything we have. Giving a one lump-sum at the end of the year to the church does not require any ongoing faith, trust or direction from God. God wants us to live by faith every day in all our choices (Proverbs 3:6; 2 Corinthians 5:7).

If you have not been practicing this principle of regular giving, now is the time to begin. Trust God and His Word. Make giving to your local church a fresh priority. Give consistently and regularly and see how God blesses you in new ways as a result.

Give from Your Firstfruits

Proverbs 3:9-10 says, "Honor the LORD with your wealth, with the first-fruits of all your crops; then your barns will be filled to overflowing, and your vats will brim over with new wine." According to this verse, we honor God when we give to Him. To "honor" God means to "give" to Him. And we are to give from our "wealth." To give from your "crops" or from your "produce" means to give from your income. Giving from our income honors God or shows due respect, praise and thanksgiving to Him for all that He has given us. When we fail to give to God we dishonor Him.

The next thing to note here is that we are to give God the "firstfruits" of our income. That means we are to give to Him "off the top." The "firstfruits" were the first crops gathered in at harvest time (Deuteronomy 26:1-11). They were the first in a series of more to come. This verse is telling us that every time we produce income we need to honor God by first giving to Him from what we have produced. That means with every paycheck I get, when I cash it, the first thing I am going to do is give some money to God. The amount is not the issue—it's the priority of giving to God first that matters. That means with every source of financial income I receive, God becomes the priority in how I spend it. I will consider Him before any other thing, be it a bill I need to pay or a desired item I've been longing to buy.

This verse also says we are to give the firstfruits from "all" our income. If it's a check of $50 from a birthday card, a check of $500 from your weekly pay, or $5,000 from cashing in on your stock options, God wants you to honor Him from the top of ALL your income. The beauty of the principle in Proverbs 3:9-10 is that it is timeless, and it can apply to anyone on a practical level. No matter how much or how often you get paid—be it daily, weekly, monthly or on commission—you can always fulfill this command of God by giving to Him from the firstfruits of your income.

I have counseled Christians who have told me they have gone months and even years without giving to the church because of their financial hardships. The excuses abound. They typically say something like, "Well, I'm going to start giving to God regularly when I'm done paying off my credit cards, or when the economy is better, or when work picks up, or when my stocks turn around, or at the end of the month or the end of the year when I'm sure I can pay all my bills." This is backwards thinking. God said give to Him from the "first" of "all" your income. Every time you make a dime, think of how you will first give Him a penny. Think later about what you'll do with what's left over.

I have had unemployed Christians tell me, "I'm not tithing right now because I'm out of work." "Well, how are you living and eating?"

I ask. They say, "Oh, well I collect unemployment...only $640 a month." And then I say, "Well, that sounds like income to me. Maybe you should start honoring God by giving to Him first thing every time you get your unemployment check."

Some people ask, "Well, what is 'income'?" The answer is simple— anytime you collect money, whether it's a gift, an earned check, a tax return, a fortuitous inheritance, a social security check, an unemployment check, profit from the sale of a house, whatever it is, honor God with your money. He will bless you in return if you obey. That's the promise of Proverbs 3:10.

If we faithfully honor God by always giving to Him from the firstfruits of all our income then He will reward us. Proverbs 3:10 says He will fill our barns to the point of "overflowing" and that our vats will brim over with new wine. (A vat is a large tub for holding liquid that is being manufactured) These are poetic expressions saying that God will meet all of our basic needs with great abundance when we honor Him with our money by making Him the priority. He is in control of all things anyway. He gives the power to make wealth. So He can providentially orchestrate all the variables and vicissitudes of life in order to fulfill His promise here where He says He will ensure that you are "brimming over" and flooded with the essentials of life. The bottom line is, "Do you trust God at His Word?"

The Bible is filled with such promises from God. King David boldly asserted, "I was young and now I am old, yet I have never seen the righteous forsaken or their children begging for bread" (Psalm 37:25). Hebrews 13:5-6 says, "Keep your lives free from the love of money and be content with what you have, because God has said, 'Never will I leave you; never will I forsake you'." The Scripture also says, "God will meet all your needs according to his glorious riches in Christ Jesus" (Philippians 4:19). Paul writes this verse in the context of money and giving. Jesus Himself affirmed that God would graciously meet all of our financial and material needs when we make Him the priority in our lives. He said, "seek first his kingdom and his righteousness, and all these things will be given to you as well" (Matthew 6:33). The "these things" Jesus refers to includes food, clothing, and shelter (vv. 25-32).

My wife and I have found this biblical principle about giving to be one of the most exciting promises God has made. During our marriage we have committed to give God from the first of all our income, from the early days when I was making $5.95 an hour scrubbing toilets as a janitor when I was in seminary. We have never had a lot of money because, unfortunately for my wife, she married a very poor college student. As we have sought to honor God by giving to Him first, He has faithfully blessed us. We have never been begging bread; always been able to pay our bills; and we have enjoyed periodic and timely financial and material blessings from God over the years. He has filled our barns with plenty.

Remember that Proverbs 3:10 does not dictate how much to give to God. That point is secondary. God is not so much interested in *how much* you give as He cares about *how* you give. Do you give the "firstfruits" of "all" your income to Him? He would rather have one dollar off the top of every paycheck than get $5,000 at the end of the year if you have failed to acknowledge Him in the previous eleven months. He wants to be first in our lives at all times, in all things, including our finances. Jesus said, "No one can serve two masters. Either he will hate the one and love the other, or he will be devoted to the one and despise the other. You cannot serve both God and money" (Matthew 6:24).

If giving to God from the first of all your income has not been a regular part of your Christian walk then now is the time to begin. It will take a step of faith on your part. You'll have to dramatically change the way you deal with money. But it will revolutionize your finances and your relationship with Him. You will encounter new kinds of blessings, assurance and fulfillment you never knew before. It may at first seem scary or uncomfortable, but in time you will realize that the safest place in the world is in the realm of obedience.

Give Willingly

When we give to the church, God wants us to do it with a willing heart. Giving should be a joyful and fulfilling act. Paul speaks directly to this attitude in 2 Corinthians where he commends the Macedonian Christians for their generous giving and tells the Corinthians they should follow suit. Paul delineates several principles of giving by the Macedonians that every Christian should consider.

As a sacrifice

First, the Macedonians gave sacrificially. Paul notes that they gave despite their "extreme poverty" (8:2). Christians frequently give excuses as to why they don't give regularly. A common one is, "Well, I don't have much income right now." That did not stop the Macedonians who were in the midst of severe poverty. We Americans don't live in extreme poverty, so we can't even imagine the implications of this statement regarding the Macedonians' plight. So don't make excuses.

With a generous heart

Second, the Macedonians gave generously. Even though they were poverty-stricken they gave to God "in rich generosity" (8:2). Paul testifies they gave "as much as they were able, and even beyond their ability" (8:3). They trusted that God would meet their needs, so they gave in an unrestrained manner—generously. They knew that you cannot out give God. This is reminiscent of the kind of sacrificial, generous giving that Jesus showcased in the account of the widow's offering:

> *Jesus sat down opposite the place where the offerings were put and watched the crowd putting their money into the temple treasury. Many rich people threw in large amounts. But a poor widow came and put in two very small copper coins, worth only a fraction of a penny. Calling his disciples to him, Jesus said, "I tell you the truth, this poor widow has put more into the treasury than all the others. They all gave out of their wealth, but she, out of her poverty, put in everything—all she had to live on" (Mark 12:41-44).*

Here Jesus praises the widow not for how much she gave, but for how she gave. She gave sacrificially, generously, willingly, out of her poverty. Jesus is accentuating the importance and priority of giving with the right attitude. Humans invariably focus on the exterior—the dollar amount. God considers what is most important—the heart and attitude. "The LORD does not look at the things man looks at. Man looks at the outward appearance, but the LORD looks at the heart" (1 Samuel 16:7).

With joy

Third, the Macedonians gave joyfully. Even though they lived in extreme poverty they had "overflowing joy" when they gave to the church (2 Corinthians 8:2). The joy they had came from God as a gift. Inner joy is one of the fruits of the Spirit that God produces in our soul when we obey Him (Galatians 5:22). I know some Christians who are lacking in joy, who are discontent, sour, easily embittered and who specialize in complaining. And many times they complain about money and the lack of it. Their Ebenezer attitude is often commensurate with or a by-product of their stingy attitude about money. They don't habitually give to God regularly, sacrificially or generously. So they miss out on God's reward of sweet inner joy and contentment.

Paul comments further on this in 2 Corinthians 9: "Each man should give what he has decided in his heart to give, not reluctantly or under compulsion, for God loves a cheerful giver" (v. 7). God loves a "cheerful giver." The Greek word here for "cheerful" is where we get our English word "hilarious" and it speaks of a willing, winsome, joyful, non-reluctant spirit of giving. It speaks of giving freely and in an uninhibited manner. God "loves" that kind of attitude! If your giving is characterized by legalistic, persnickety, tight-fisted, apprehensive second-guessing and regrets, then God is not going to be pleased with your giving.

As an act of worship

Fourth, the Macedonians gave worshipfully. These exemplary Christians knew that giving money to the church, or "to the saints" (2 Corinthians 8:4), was not an exercise in self-serving philanthropic, government-oriented, tax-deductible charity. First and foremost, their giving was an act of worship. It was a voluntary expression of thanksgiving to God for all that He had done for them (9:11). Paul says "they gave themselves first to the Lord" (8:5). They gave financially to God and the church because they knew God first gave all things to them (1 John 4:19), the most important thing being total forgiveness of sins through the sacrificial death of Christ: "For you know the grace of our Lord Jesus Christ, that though He was rich, yet for your sakes he became poor, so that you through His poverty might become rich" (8:9).

The above verse, more than any other, provides us as Christians with the ultimate motive for giving to God and the church. We give as an act of worship and thanksgiving to tangibly show God, as an expression of faith, that we owe all good things to Him—the greatest of which is salvation in Jesus Christ. We don't give to the church primarily because we gotta' get those bills paid, or because we need to meet the budget, or because we gotta finish that building project, or because we gotta pay off the balance of that loan, or because we need new carpet in the nursery. We give because it is an act of worship, as everything we do in life should be. As the Scripture says, "so whether you eat or drink or whatever you do [including how you handle your money], do it all for the glory of God" (1 Corinthians 10:31).

With discernment

Fifth, the Macedonians gave wisely. They were discerning and careful stewards of their money. They did not give indiscriminately to anyone who asked. That would be unwise and poor stewardship of God's resources. This world is filled with people begging for handouts and making illegitimate and deceptive pleas for money (2 Timothy 3:1-2; 2 Peter 2:1, 13-14). Don't be fooled. Know who you are giving to. The Macedonians did. They gave to Paul and the church because they knew Paul was a conscientious, careful and reliable steward of the saints' money and resources. They entrusted their collection to those in the church who had established and proven credibility. Integrity and fiscal responsibility were priorities for Paul and the Macedonians. Paul describes the careful procedures and precautions taken in collecting the saints' money:

> ...we carry the offering, which we administer in order to honor the Lord himself and to show our eagerness to help. We want to avoid any criticism of the way we administer this liberal gift. For we are taking pains to do what is right, not only in the eyes of the Lord but also in the eyes of men (2 Corinthians 8:19-20).

Don't give thoughtlessly to anyone holding out his hand. Remember Proverbs 3:9 that said "honor the LORD" with your wealth. Giving to wrong causes and wrong people and for wrong reasons does not honor God.

So who should Christians be giving to? Here are some priorities to keep in mind. Give first to the local church. Give where you are being spiritually fed (1 Corinthians 9:7-14). Some Christians say, "I give to other charitable organizations," or "I give to this parachurch organization, etc." Giving to other good causes is legitimate, but not when that giving supplants or takes away from giving to the local church. Jesus promised to build His "church" (Matthew 16:18). The church is the Body of Christ, an eternal entity—every other organization is temporal, man-made and second-fiddle to God's church (Acts 20:28; 1 Timothy 3:15).

Also, give to the appropriate leadership of the local church. This is the New Testament model. The early Christians "brought the money...and put it at the apostles' feet, and it was distributed to anyone as he had need" (Acts 4:34-35; cf. v. 37). The church leaders are the God-ordained stewards responsible for collecting and distributing the church offering (Romans 13:1-2). "They are representatives of the churches and an honor to Christ" (2 Corinthians 8:23).

But some Christians want to give "designated gifts" instead of giving into the general offering. They say this is because they don't trust people or the bureaucracy of the process. They want to be sure their money is used for what they intended. But that is not their responsibility. If you don't trust the leadership of your church, then go to a church you can trust (1 Corinthians 16:3-4). The leaders of the church are accountable to God regarding their stewardship of the church's finances (1 Corinthians 4:1-5; James 3:1), your responsibility is to give according to the established pattern laid down by God in the Scriptures and trust Him for the results.

With confidence

Sixth, the Macedonians gave confidently. They knew God would bless them for their sacrificial, generous, wise giving. God's grace prompted the Macedonians' right attitude regarding giving (2 Corinthians 8:1). They knew that giving to the church was a divine "privilege" (8:4). They knew they were giving according to "God's will" (8:5). They knew their act of giving was an act of love that would bless others who were in need (8:13-15). They were "zealous" and had "enthusiasm" in giving to God (8:22; 9:2).

Why did the Macedonians give with confident zeal and enthusiasm in the midst of their severe poverty? Paul tells us. They knew an inviolable spiritual secret about giving—an eternal axiomatic law established by God: "Remember this: Whoever sows sparingly will also reap sparingly, and whoever sows generously will also reap generously" (9:6). What an amazing promise! God has said that if you are financially generous toward Him and His church, then He will be generous with you. If you are stingy with God, then He will be stingy with you. Jesus taught this very thing about money. Paul echoes the words of Jesus when he reminded the elders at the church of Ephesus:

> *In everything I did, I showed you that by this kind of hard work we must help the weak, remembering the words the Lord Jesus himself said: 'It is more blessed to give than to receive"* (Acts 20:35).

Here Jesus says that when you give you will be greatly blessed. When you are stingy, or withhold a gift, or give grudgingly or under compulsion, you lose out on the blessings of God. Jesus elaborates on the details of these blessings in Luke 6:

> *Give, and it will be given to you. A good measure, pressed down, shaken together and running over, will be poured into your lap. For with the measure you use, it will be measured to you* (v. 38).

Jesus is saying that when we give generously, then God will give back to us generously. And when He gives back to us, He does so magnanimously. The imagery above is taken from the grain fields when grain was carried in the lap of one's robe. The grain was pressed down and packed air-tight to the point of overflowing. The point is that God is not going to be chintzy and gyp you like the potato chip people do when they give you a bag full of air with a few crumbs in the bottom of the bag, or the stingy ice cream guy who does not fill your whole cone up with ice cream, but just puts a lump on the top. So give generously. If you do, God will give generously to you. If you sow generously, you will reap the same. You can't out-give God.

The Truth about "Tithing"

There is widespread confusion and misunderstanding about "tithing" among church people. Christian churches abroad ascribe to "tithing" as the universal, binding pattern of biblically required giving for the Church. There are innumerable books and sermons commanding Christians to pay their required ten percent to God or else... To bunker the threat, these teachers usually throw out the sobering warning of Malachi 3:8-10, which says the following:

> *"Will a man rob God? Yet you rob me. But you ask, 'How do we rob you?' In tithes and offerings. You are under a curse—the whole nation of you—because you are robbing me. Bring the whole tithe into the storehouse, that there may be food in my house. Test me in this," says the LORD Almighty," and see if I will not throw open the floodgates of heaven and pour out so much blessing that you will not have room enough for it."*

Admittedly, this is the ideal passage to use if you want to manipulate people and scare them into coughing up the money. But the problem is that this passage is not a binding mandate on the church or on Christians today. This rebuke is spoken by God to the theocracy of Israel regarding their main required tithes laid down in the Mosaic law intended for sustaining the Old Testament religious system (Numbers 18:25-30; Deuteronomy 12:10-11; 17-18; 14:28-29). But the church is not the Old Testament theocracy of Israel. So how does the "tithe" relate to the Church today and to Christians? Consider the following principles from Scripture.

First of all, the word "tithe" means "a tenth." Surprisingly, the New Testament never commands the Church or Christians to give a "tithe" or a tenth of their income! That is hard to believe in the light of the preponderance of teaching in churches commanding the church to "bring ye in the tithe!" There are many evangelical churches that even require, as a condition of church membership, their people to give ten percent of all their income. But that is not biblical. This mandatory "tithing" notion is a classic example of human tradition and man-made religion creeping into the church, supplanting and smothering out the simplicity of God's true requirements. Jesus warned His disciples of this human tendency to obscure biblical truth with spiritualize and legalistic counterfeits:

He replied, "Isaiah was right when he prophesied about you hypocrites: as it is written: 'These people honor me with their lips, but their hearts are far from me. They worship me in vain; their teachings are but rules taught by men.' You have let go of the commands of God and are holding on the traditions of men." And he said to them, "You have a fine way of setting aside the commands of God in order to observe your own traditions!...Thus you nullify the word of God by your tradition that you have handed down. And you do many things like that" (Mark 7:6-9; 13).

"Woe to you, teachers of the law and Pharisees, you hypocrites! You give a tenth of your spices—mint, dill and cummin. But you have neglected the more important matters of the law—justice, mercy and faithfulness. You should have practiced the latter, without neglecting the former. You blind guides! You strain out a gnat but swallow a camel" (Matthew 23:23-24).

Second of all, Jesus never commanded the church to give a tenth and the apostles never commanded Christians to give a tenth to the church. The New Testament passages that address giving in the church don't mention a "tithe" (see 1 Corinthians 9, 16; 2 Corinthians 8-9; Philippians 4, etc.). Yet the New Testament delineates very clearly God's expectation for giving in the church. It has already been shown above what that pattern is: God expects the Christian to give to the church from the heart, from the first fruits, generously, sacrificially, wisely, willingly and with joy and confidence as an act of worship. A legalistic, mandated expectation of forking over strictly ten percent—no more, no less—undermines biblical teaching and is contrary to God's established pattern.

Third, a strict "tithing" procedure actually circumvents and inhibits biblical giving. Consider some of its shortcomings. "Tithing" requires no faith. You get your check, you do the math, you cut the check—no faith required. No prayerful consideration necessary. No pleading with God for divine wisdom needed. Just do the math and cut the check. On the contrary, biblical giving is more intimate, personal, worshipful and dependent upon God's leading. With every paycheck we should ask God to give us wisdom (James 1:5), to prompt our hearts, to show us the needs, and to bless our giving, whatever the amount. The priority in this scenario is the human heart. This is "freewill" giving which God has always expected from His people. Notice an example even from the days of Moses and the Law:

> Moses said to the whole Israelite community, "This is what the LORD has commanded: From what you have, take an offering for the LORD. **Everyone who is willing** is to bring to the LORD an offering of gold, silver and bronze..." (Exodus 35:4-5).

> And **everyone who was willing and whose heart moved him** came and brought an offering to the LORD for the work on the Tent of Meeting, for all its service and all its sacred garments. **All who were willing,** men and women alike, came and brought gold jewelry of all kinds...All the Israelite men and women **who were willing** brought to the LORD **freewill offerings** for all the work the LORD through Moses had commanded them to do (Exodus 35:21-22; 29).

> So all the skilled craftsmen who were doing all the work on the sanctuary left their work and said to Moses, "The people are bringing more than enough for doing the work the LORD commanded to be done." Then Moses gave an order and sent this word throughout the camp: "No man or woman is to make anything else as an offering for the sanctuary." And so the people were restrained from bringing more, because what they already had was more than enough to do all the work (Exodus 36:4-6).

What an incredible story. The people were not coerced or manipulated into giving—only those who were willing had to give. And the people gave so generously to the work of the LORD that they received too much! Moses had to tell them to stop giving. When was the last time that happened in any Christian church? But this is the biblical model of giving—from the heart, those who are willing. Remember the godly Macedonians who gave sacrificially "entirely on their own" (2 Corinthians

8:3). They gave a freewill offering. Similarly, Paul said every Christian "should give what he has decided in his [own] heart to give, not reluctantly or under compulsion, for God loves a cheerful [hilarious] giver" (9:7). Even the few times that tithing is mentioned in Genesis, before the giving of the Law, it was an act of spontaneous, freewill giving—not a timeless, binding mandate for all people for all time (see Genesis 14:17-20; cf. Hebrews 7:4; Genesis 28:20-22).

A final thought about tithing to consider is that a mandatory tithe of ten percent can be limiting—it actually can inhibit giving. What if I want to give fifteen or twenty percent or more? Ah, no need, you already filled your rigid quota. On the contrary, it was the freedom in giving that prompted the Israelites to give to the full, so much so that they gave too much. Maybe we are stifling the giving of the saints in our churches by prescribing legalistic practices that fail to fully honor God?

In sum, the Bible does talk about "tithing," but its use is frequently misunderstood and distorted in the church. God used the tithe in both a voluntary and compulsory manner to manage and sustain the theocracy of the Israelite religious community. The church is never told to "tithe" ten percent. Christians are expected to give freewill offerings from the first fruits, regularly, sacrificially, wisely and with joy and confidence as an act of thanksgiving and worship to God because of the saving work of the Lord and Savior Jesus Christ.

Questions for Review

1. Give a Bible verse that teaches God owns everything:

_____

_____

_____

2. Read Acts 4:32-35; what was the attitude of the early disciples toward money and possession?

_____

_____

_____

_____

3. What are some practical implications of Deuteronomy 8:18, which says, "God is the one who gives you the power to produce wealth"?

_____

_____

_____

_____

4. What does it mean to "give from your first fruits"?

_____

_____

_____

_____

5. Does God care most about how much we give? What is most important about biblical giving?

_____

_____

_____

_____

6. What does it mean that God loves a "cheerful giver" (2 Corinthians 9:7)?

_____

_____

_____

_____

7. Where does the New Testament command Christians to give a tithe"?

_____

_____

_____

_____

8. What does "tithe" literally mean?

_____

_____

_____

_____

9. Evaluate your own giving pattern. Are you giving regularly to the local church? If so, how often? If not, why not, and how can you begin to do so immediately?

_____

_____

_____

_____

10. According to Scripture, what are some of the ways God will bless you if you give regularly and generously to His Church?

_____

_____

_____

_____

For further study on Give! **see these helpful resources:**
The Treasure Principle, by Randy Alcorn
Master Your Money, by Ron Blue
Gifts from the Heart, by Larry Burkett
Your Money Counts, by Howard Dayton
Giving to God, by David Jeremiah
Whose Money is it Anyway?, by John MacArthur
The Grace of Giving, by Stephen Olford

7

Go!

"Go into all the world and preach the good news to all creation"
(Mark 16:15)

When you became a Christian you inherited countless spiritual blessings including adoption into God's family, total forgiveness of sins, the indwelling Holy Spirit, eternal life, protection from the Devil, deliverance from death and hell, just to name a few. All these blessings are included in the term "salvation." God gave you the gift of salvation. And in turn God wants you to tell others about this gift. As a matter of fact, He doesn't just want you to tell others, He commands it. All Christians are commanded to proclaim the message of salvation—to share their faith.

This obligation to share the faith with others is commonly referred to as "evangelism." The Bible gives several guidelines to the Christian on how to effectively "evangelize" unbelievers.

The Great Comission

The best place to start is with the "Great Commission" that Jesus gave to His disciples before He ascended into heaven after His resurrection. It is found in Matthew 28:16-20 and it says,

> *Then the eleven disciples went to Galilee, to the mountain*
> *where Jesus had told them to go. When they saw him, they*

worshipped him; but some doubted. Then Jesus came to them and said, "All authority in heaven and on earth has been given to me. Therefore go and make disciples of all nations, baptizing them in the name of the Father and of the Son and of the Holy Spirit, and teaching them to obey everything I have commanded you. And surely I am with you always, to the very end of the age."

This passage is referred to as the "Great Commission" for good reasons. First of all it's a "commission," meaning it is an obligation given by someone in authority. In this case, Jesus is the one who has the authority. Second of all, this commission is "great" for it is a major priority for the church. And every Christian is part of the church. So every Christian should make a priority of the Great Commission.

The main imperative or command in the Great Commission is "to make disciples." A "disciple" in the New Testament is a dedicated follower and student of Jesus.

According to this passage, Christians are to make disciples by "going," "baptizing," and "teaching"—and in that order. In verses 19-20, these three words in the Greek language are participles and they all modify the main verb, "make disciples." "Make disciples" is literally one word in the original language.

"Going" emphasizes the truth that Christians are to infiltrate the world with God's truth by way of their words and their lifestyle. They are to be Christ's witnesses wherever they go. The Bible says we are "ambassadors" (2 Corinthians 5:20). An ambassador is someone formally appointed to represent another. God has appointed us to represent Him wherever we go—at home, with the relatives, with the neighbors, on the job, to the mailman, to the checker at the supermarket, to the barber, with the waitress at the restaurant.

Christians are not to be isolationists, cloistered in holy huddles, snobbishly eschewing any interaction with those in the world. Just the opposite is true—they are supposed to "go," "go," "go"! The church is not a cul-de-sac, narcissisticly hoarding the truth; rather, it is a channel called to pour out the waters of God's love to the whole world. That's what Mark 16:15 says—"*Go* into all the world..."!

Evaluate your own mindset and lifestyle for a moment in light of this truth—the truth that if you are a Christian you are supposed to be sharing Christ wherever you go—all the time, with everyone. It's a sobering and convicting obligation. But it's not impossible.

If it sounds impossible or too intimidating, then the place to start is with prayer. Ask God specifically to give you the desire and boldness to share your faith wherever you go. Also ask God to provide specific opportunities to do it. It is His will, so He will definitely bring opportunities your way. We must first be willing.

Paul prayed that way. He said, "Pray also for me, that whenever I open my mouth, words may be given [to] me so that I will fearlessly make known the mystery of the gospel, for which I am an ambassador" (Ephesians 6:19-20). If the great Apostle Paul needed prayer to overcome fear at the prospect of evangelizing the lost, how much more do we need prayer?

As we make "going" a part of our everyday lifestyle, then inevitably some people we talk to will become Christians. That leads to the second step in the Great Commission which is "baptizing." This second step simply refers to encouraging new believers to formally identify with the local church by committing to baptism and church membership. In this second step they give public testimony to their new found faith.

The third step in the Great Commission is "teaching." Once someone has heard the gospel from our "going," and after that person has believed and joined the church through "baptizing," then the local church has the responsibility of helping the new church member grow in his faith. We do this by "teaching" the new disciple. The content of what we teach him is "everything" Jesus shared and left with His apostles— all of which can be found in the Bible.

For further information about "baptizing" and "teaching" you can refer to the chapters "Join!" and "Disciple!" in this book.

The Last Commission

In addition to the Great Commission, the "Last Commission" Jesus gave to His disciples is paramount when it comes to sharing the Christian faith with others. In the military they say the most important command that the general gives when an army is at war is the last command that the general gives. Christians are in a spiritual war, and the last command that our Commander-In-Chief gave to the Church is in Acts 1:8, which says,

But you will receive power when the Holy Spirit comes on you; and you will be My witnesses in Jerusalem, and in all Judea and Samaria, and to the ends of the earth.

These words that Jesus gave to His disciples just prior to His ascension into heaven further clarify Jesus' command in Matthew 28. In the present passage He emphasizes *how* the Church is to fulfill the Great Commission.

The Holy Spirit must lead

First, Jesus reveals that Christians can't share their faith effectively without the help of the "Holy Spirit." The moment you became a Christian the Holy Spirit literally came to live inside you—the third Person of the Trinity took up residence in your heart. This is what Paul means when he says that the moment you trusted Christ you were "sealed...with the Holy Spirit of promise" (Ephesians 1:13, NASB).

So all Christians have the Holy Spirit living in them. And Paul elsewhere says that if you don't have the Holy Spirit living in you then you are not a Christian (Romans 8:9). And once the Holy Spirit comes to live in you at the point of salvation, then He will never leave you—not until you die and go to be with God in heaven or until Jesus returns! (Hebrews 13:5)

In Acts 1:8 Jesus is reminding believers that they must rely totally on the power and leading of the Holy Spirit when it comes to sharing the gospel. We do this by obeying the Holy Spirit Whose words are revealed in the Bible, by praying to the Holy Spirit asking for His help, guidance, comfort and wisdom, and by being patient—allowing Him to providentially lead and create opportunities for sharing. We can't be juggernauts and steamrollers, shoving the truth down people's throats apart from God's leading. Read Acts 16:6-7 for an example of Paul being sensitive to the specific leading of God's Spirit in his evangelistic endeavors.

Give your testimony

Another principle in Acts 1:8 comes from Jesus' words when He says, "you shall be my witnesses." When we have an opportunity to talk with people about religious matters, we should give our testimony of how He saved us.

The Greek word for "witnesses" is literally "martyrs." Originally a martyr was an eyewitness who gave legal testimony in a court of law under the penalty of death. And the emphasis was on a testimony given from a personal experience and personal involvement regarding the issue at hand. That is how Christians are supposed to witness for Christ. They are to tell the truth, the whole truth, and nothing but the truth of how Jesus came into their lives and saved them from their sins. And they are supposed to tell how He did it—even in the face of rejection, scorn, harm or death!

Giving your testimony is easy actually, because you are talking about the most familiar thing in the world...you! When sharing your testimony, emphasize how God has changed you. Give specific examples of how He supernaturally made you a new person.

As for me, I think of when I first got saved in college at age nineteen. For many years as an unbeliever I had a gutter-mouth—saying bad words came naturally. I could use one cuss word as all eight parts of speech in one sentence quite naturally. Then about a month after I had been saved I noticed that I had not said a cuss word in about a month—which coincided with the very time I had become a Christian.

As a young Christian that was a dramatic sign and confirmation of how God had come into my life and changed me. He made me a new person at salvation. He first cleaned up my heart, which in turn cleaned out my mouth. Not only did I not cuss anymore—I no longer had the desire to. This great life-changing experience is exactly what Scripture says happens to someone when they get saved: "Therefore, if anyone is in Christ, he is a new creation; the old has gone, the new has come!" (2 Corinthians 5:17).

Begin in your own backyard

A third principle about evangelism from Acts 1:8 has to do with strategy. Jesus says when you share your faith with others, begin "in Jerusalem." In effect, Jesus is saying that to be an effective witness for Him you need to start in your own backyard. Start small, where you are. Grow where you are planted. You don't have to go to Timbuktu to be a faithful witness for Christ. God wants witnesses and missionaries right where you are.

Begin to cultivate relationships with the people immediately around you—at home, in the family, in your neighborhood, your place of employment, where you exercise, etc. Then begin to pray for those unbelievers around you by name, asking God to open their hearts so they are receptive to the gospel and asking for opportunities to share the truth with them. Over time you'll see that if you are faithful in the small things, then God will give you greater things. Focus on the depth of your ministry to people, and let God worry about the breadth of it.

Do you know the names of the neighbors to the right and left of your house? Do you know your mailman's name? Do the people at your work know you are a follower of Christ? Do they know what that means? When was the last time you shared the gospel with someone? When was the first or last time you prayed with someone to receive Christ? Unfortunately I have met and talked with many Christians who have never shared the gospel with an unbeliever—even after being a Christian themselves for five, ten, twenty years! Unthinkable. Christians are supposed to be in the business of sharing the Christian faith all the time, everywhere they go, with everyone they meet. We need a wake-up call.

See the bigger picture

After concentrating on Jerusalem, Jesus said to then focus on "Judea and Samaria, and to the ends of the earth." We are supposed to begin where we are, but our evangelistic mindset should not stop there. In this passage Jesus is saying that every Christian should have a universal perspective when it comes to the lost. Christ's goal is the world! "To the uttermost part of the earth."

So while focusing on local evangelism, every Christian can be giving toward and regularly praying for world evangelism. You can do that in a few ways. One way is to financially support a Christian missionary out on the field somewhere else in the world. In all the years of our marriage my wife and I have always tried to support at least one missionary abroad that we knew and trusted. That has been rewarding as we have vicariously experienced the blessing of being a part of the universal aspects of Acts 1:8.

Another way to participate in the universal component of Acts 1:8 is to go on a short-term mission. This can be a life-changing experience for every Christian. I know it was for my wife who was able to go on a sixteen-day mission trip to Cambodia with our home church.

She had a wonderful experience helping construct a church building for national Christians there, as well as sharing the love of Christ with hundreds of Cambodian children. Her faith was stretched and strengthened by being forced out of her comfort zone in many ways, from the foreign menu to the lack of modern conveniences. Being a busy mother of four young children, it was a practical and unique way to be a part of global missions as Jesus commanded in Acts 1:8.

What is the Gospel?

The Gospel is a specific message

We have seen above what Jesus expects from the church and from every Christian—we are supposed to be sharing the gospel wherever we go. But what is the "gospel" we are supposed to be sharing with the lost world? Surprisingly, there is great confusion in the church about that most basic issue. This is tragic, for no one is saved apart from hearing and believing in the gospel. That's what the Bible says. Consider the following Scriptures that speak to this issue:

> *I am not ashamed of the gospel, because it is the power of God for the salvation of everyone who believes (Romans 1:16).*
> *For you have been born again, not of perishable seed, but of imperishable, through the living and enduring word of God...And this is the word that was preached to you (1 Peter 1:23, 25).*
> *How, then, can they call on the one they have not believed in? And how can they believe in the one of whom they have not heard? And how can they hear without someone preaching to them? And how can they preach unless they are sent? As it is written, "How beautiful are the feet of those who bring good news!" (Romans 10:14-15).*

Maybe some Christians are confused on this matter, but the Bible is crystal clear as to what the gospel is. Paul clearly defines the saving gospel in 1 Corinthians 15:1-4:

> *Now, brothers, I want to remind you of **the gospel** I preached to you, which you received and on which you have taken your stand. By this gospel you are saved, if you hold firmly to the word I preached to you. Otherwise, you have believed in vain. For what I received I passed on to you as of first importance: that Christ died for our sins according to the Scriptures, that he was buried, that he was raised on the third day according to the Scriptures, and that he appeared to Peter, and then to the Twelve.*

Here in verse one Paul reminds the Corinthians of "the gospel." In verse two he says it was through "this gospel" that they were "saved." In verses three and four he summarizes the contents of the gospel.

The gospel is good news

Before getting to the content of verses three and four, it is imperative to first define the word "gospel." In the New Testament this word refers to a specific message about the saving life and death of Jesus Christ. The "gospel" does not refer to the whole Bible as many people wrongly believe. The "gospel" does not refer to the first four books of the New Testament as others naively think. The "gospel" is more specific and precise than that.

The Greek word for "gospel" is *euanngelion* which is a compound word made up of two words, *eu* = "good" + *anngelos* = "message." This compound word is the basis for our English word, "ev-angelism." "Evangelism" is the process of sharing the "good message" or "good news" with unbelievers. That's why our English Bibles sometimes translate variants of this Greek word as "gospel," "good news" or as "evangelist."

The implication from the above truth is that Christians are supposed to be bringing "good news" or a message of "hope" to unbelievers. Unfortunately, some misguided Christians bring a one-sided message of only doom and gloom to the lost.

I have met Christians who have told me that the gospel can be summed up with the following statement: "You are a sinner worthy of God's eternal hell and wrath, and all your human acts of righteousness are nothing but filthy rags in His sight."

I have pointed out to such short-sighted Christian misers that their message has no "good news" in it whatsoever, no message of hope for the sinner, no component of God's love and mercy, not to mention that the person of Jesus Christ was totally left out! That is no gospel at all! That is only half the message. We need to give the complete gospel—the holiness of God in addition to His love, mercy and compassion.

The gospel is about who Jesus is

That takes us back to 1 Corinthians 15. Paul makes it clear that the gospel is all about "Christ" (verse 3)—who He is, what He did, and why He did it.

The "gospel" begins with who Jesus is. Paul calls Him "Christ," which means Jesus is "the Anointed One." "Christ" is the New Testament word for the Old Testament "Messiah." Paul declares that Jesus is the Old Testament Messiah.

The Old Testament says the Messiah is the only Savior of the world (Isaiah 43:11), equal with YHWH God (Psalm 45:6-7; Heb 1:8), the LORD of Heaven (Psalm 110:1), eternal (Isaiah 9:6), the sinless Holy One (Isaiah 6:3), worthy of worship (Psalm 2:12), all-powerful (Isaiah 44:6), all-knowing (Isaiah 46:10) and the Judge of every soul (Psalm 2:12). That's who Jesus is!

And that is what we are supposed to share with unbelievers—we are telling them first and foremost about a Person. And they must know who Jesus is before they can commit to Him. This is what Jesus meant when He said, "Now this is eternal life: that they may know you, the only true God, and Jesus Christ, whom you have sent" (John 17:3).

Before you marry someone, you need to get to know who that person really is—the same is true about becoming a Christian. Before being wed to Christ, you first must know who He is. He's not just a good man as modern moralists try to tell us as they marginalize His Deity. He's not just a good prophet as Islam tries to tell us. He's not just one of many lesser gods like Mormonism tries to tell us. He's not just one way to heaven among many ways as Hinduism tries to tell us.

Jesus is the Lord, God, and the only way to heaven. Romans 10:9-10 says, "If you confess with your mouth Jesus as Lord...you shall be saved." Acts 16:31 says, "Believe in the Lord Jesus and you shall be saved." Jesus said that He was "the way, the truth, and the life; no one comes to the Father" except through Him (John 14:6). So as you share the good news of Jesus Christ with unbelievers wherever you go, start by telling them clearly, and thoroughly, who Jesus is.

The gospel is about the meaning of Jesus' death

After telling people who Jesus is, then focus on what Jesus did. First Corinthians 15 says Jesus "died for our sins." The death of Christ is the heart of the gospel. This is why Jesus came to earth. It's why He was born—Jesus came to die. His death was no accident, nor the result of a failed and botched plan. His death was purposed, orchestrated and carried out according to God's own plan down to the last grisly detail.

Jesus' death may have been a surprise to many in His day, but it was no surprise to Him. He predicted His death the day before He died (John 13), several months before (Matthew 17:22-23), a year before (Matthew 16:21), and even three years before His death (John 2:19). Luke 2:35 predicted His death thirty-three years before it happened. Isaiah 53 predicted Jesus' substitutionary death 700 years before it came to pass. Amazingly, Psalm 22:16 predicted Jesus the Messiah would die by crucifixion 1,000 years ahead of time. Genesis 3:15 predicted the Messiah would die 4,000 years before it happened. All this was possible because God the Father planned the death of Christ in eternity past, before the world was ever created (Acts 2:23)!

The death of Christ is referred to over 170 times in the New Testament. So it is the central feature of Christianity. It's central because of its significance. Paul says Jesus died "for...sins." The fact that Jesus died for our sins is complex and multi-faceted and includes the following blessed truths:

1. Jesus' death was a "substitution." Jesus died in our place. He was punished by God the Father so that we wouldn't have to be (Isaiah 53:5).
2. Jesus' death was a "propitiation." This means that God's holy wrath and anger was "satisfied" or "appeased" by Christ's sacrificial death, for justice against sin was satisfied (1 John 2:2, NASB).
3. Jesus' death provided our "justification." As sinners, we were guilty in God's court of law. Jesus' death satisfied the penalty and consequences of God's perfect Law, and therefore He declared us "not guilty!" (Romans 3:21-26)
4. Jesus' death accomplished "redemption." This means Jesus "purchased" us out of the slavery of sin, self and Satan with the ransom price of His blood (1 Peter 1:18-19).
5. Jesus' death provided "reconciliation." We were born separated from God because of the sin we inherited from Adam and Eve. We were literally God's enemies. Jesus' death wiped away the hostility in our relationship with God so that we could become friends with Him (Romans 5:10).
6. Jesus' death provided spiritual "adoption" on our behalf. When a person trusts in Christ's death for one's sin, that person becomes born again, eternally regenerated, at which moment he

or she is adopted into God's spiritual family as a child of God (John 1:12).

So when we share the gospel with unbelievers, we need to emphasize the *meaning* of Christ's death.

The gospel is about the reality of Jesus' resurrection

Next in 1 Corinthians 15 Paul goes on to say that after Jesus was buried, "he was raised on the third day" (verse 4). The resurrection of Jesus Christ is an indispensable part of the gospel. You cannot become a Christian apart from believing that Jesus rose from the dead. Romans 10:9 says that if "you believe in your heart that God raised" Jesus from the dead then "you will be saved." Salvation is contingent upon knowing, understanding and appropriating the significance of Christ's resurrection.

This only makes sense, for Jesus would have no power to save if He was still dead. But He is alive! He conquered death. Because He lives, we also will live (John 14:19). By rising from the grave Jesus demonstrated that He is Lord and that He has power over death, which is the inevitable consequence of sin. No other religious person in history can make such a claim—only Jesus can, and that is why only Jesus can save someone from sin, death, the world, hell and the Devil.

The truth of the resurrection was the apex of Peter and Paul's gospel presentations given in the Book of Acts as they called people to salvation in Christ (2:24; 3:15; 4:10; 5:30; 13:30; 17:31; 26:23). Resurrection truth became the defining element and unique feature for the early church. Paul declared that he was on trial because he believed in the resurrection of Jesus (Acts 23:6). Resurrection truth needs to be our clarion cry as well today as we go out to the unsaved world and proclaim the good news.

Since this is true, it should be no surprise that other religions deny, redefine, or ignore the resurrection of Christ altogether. For example, Islam—the largest religion in the world today with over one billion adherents—says that Jesus was a real man, but He never died on the cross nor did He rise from the dead. But the truth is the literal, historical, bodily resurrection of Jesus Christ is a litmus test for real spirituality that all Christians should be ready to proclaim and defend.

The gospel is a call to repent

In addition to giving the objective content of the gospel message in 1 Corinthians 15, Paul also refers to the subjective response people should have toward the message. This response on our part entails "believing" and "repenting." Repentance is negative, relating to our attitude toward sin. Believing is positive, relating to our attitude toward God.

When we share the gospel with others we have to talk about sin. After all Jesus died for "our sins" as Paul declares in verse 3. People have to know they are lost before they understand how and why to be saved. They need to know what Jesus saves people from. The bad news accentuates and puts in stark relief the good news. People need to know they have spiritual terminal cancer of the soul before we explain the antidote of the gospel to them.

This is how Jesus preached the gospel. Mark 1:14-15 says when Jesus came preaching the good news, His message was, "Repent and believe the good news!" Repentance was also at the heart of Peter's gospel preaching. In Acts 2 he told people they could be saved if they "repent...in the name of Jesus Christ so that your sins may be forgiven" (v. 38). Paul said the same thing. He declared that the gospel message he shared with unbelievers included a call to "repent and turn to God" (Acts 26:20).

In the Bible, the word "repent" simply means "to turn." It's a picturesque way of describing a person's change of heart about sin after he has been convicted by the Holy Spirit (John 16:8). Repentance is an act of the will in response to the work of God in a person's heart. It manifests itself most simply in a heartfelt prayer to God, as the sinner pleads for God's forgiveness (Luke 18:13-14). When prayed sincerely, God will honor such a prayer (Romans 10:13).

Recently, some have tried to emasculate the saving gospel by telling us that we should not ask unbelievers to repent or turn from their sin. But Jesus did and He has commanded us to do the same. Being obedient to Christ is more important than caving in to the fear of man, no matter how well-intentioned a misguided notion may be. So when you share the gospel with unbelievers, be sure to talk with them about their sin and call them to repentance.

The gospel is a call to believe

After sharing the content of the good news with people, we need to call on them to believe the message. In the Bible the word "believe" means "to trust in" or "to have faith in" and it includes an act of the will in addition to intellectual assent. In other words, a person needs to make a formal commitment to the gospel and Jesus to become a Christian.

This is basic. Paul said, "Confess with your mouth Jesus as Lord...and you shall be saved" (Romans 10:9-10). Believing is trusting in the person of God and everything He says. Believing is an attitude of trusting Jesus—following Him wherever He goes, doing whatever He requires. Jesus said this attitude of trust was a prerequisite for becoming a Christian when He proclaimed:

> *If anyone would come after me, he must deny himself and take up his cross daily and follow me. For whoever wants to save his life will lose it, but whoever loses his life for me will save it. What good is it for a man to gain the whole world, and yet lose or forfeit his very self? (Luke 9:23-25).*

Believing is not a human work. The ability to believe in the gospel is a gift from God (Ephesians 2:8-9). Like repentance, belief is an act of the will resulting from the inner working of God's Holy Spirit. Nevertheless, it is a real, subjective human response. As such, when we share the gospel with unbelievers we need to implore them to believe the message (Isaiah 55:1-7).

The gospel in a nutshell

Summing it up, the gospel we are supposed to be sharing with non-Christians entails proclaiming the specific message of good news that God has a remedy for sin that damns people's souls. That remedy is Jesus Christ.

Jesus is the all-glorious God-Man who came down from heaven, lived a perfect and sinless life, willingly died on the cross as a substitute for human sin, appeased God's wrath and provided a way for people to know God personally. Jesus demonstrated His Lordship and the right to be the only Savior by rising bodily from the dead after three days. He is alive today and reigns as King in heaven. He wants all people everywhere to turn away from their sins and put their trust in Him alone for the forgiveness of sins and to have eternal life. In order to get forgiveness from God the Father and eternal life, all one has to do is believe in this gospel—this message of good news.

Roadblocks to Going

We have seen that sharing the gospel with unbelievers is the most basic expectation God has for Christians. Nevertheless, there are many Christians who do not evangelize regularly, or at all, despite the imperative of the Great Commission. Why is that? Having pastored in four different churches for the past sixteen years I have encountered common denominators or "roadblacks" that deter Christians from fulfilling their obligation. Consider the following and make sure they are not true of you.

The fear of man

The most prevalent inhibitor that I have seen squelching evangelism among believers is 'fear'—the fear of man and the fear of rejection. No one likes to be rejected—most people want to be liked and accepted. But that is not the calling of a Christian. We are called to faithfully discharge the message of Christ and to do so boldly.

Inevitably there will be people who resist the message, who don't want to turn from their sin, follow Christ or submit to God. But the New Testament says that is a normal response from people. Jesus, the Apostles, and Paul were soundly rejected routinely, and sometimes violently. Jesus warned His disciples about this when He said categorically, "All men will hate you because of me" (Luke 21:17).

Regarding rejection from men, Peter reminded Christians, "do not be surprised at the painful trial you are suffering, as though something strange were happening to you...If you are insulted because of the name of Christ, you are blessed, for the Spirit of glory and of God rests on you" (1 Peter 4:12, 14). Paul told Christians that they are called "not only to believe on him, but also to suffer for him" (Philippians 1:29). He also said, "everyone who wants to live a godly life in Christ Jesus will be persecuted" (2 Timothy 3:12). That's a promise!

No results...apparently

Another common reason Christians don't share the gospel is because they have become discouraged. Maybe they used to share the gospel with everyone enthusiatically when they first got saved, but then were disillusioned by the lack of positive feedback and few tangible results. It is easy to cultivate a mindset in that instance that says, "It doesn't do any good—that person is never going to become a Christian."

But that is the wrong attitude. We are called to be the messengers and the seed-planters. We can't save anyone—that is God's job. We need to keep persevering by faithfully sharing the gospel and praying for the lost, no matter what the results are. God will do the harvesting in His perfect time (1 Corinthians 3:5-9).

Cold and dry

Some Christians don't share the gospel simply because they have become spiritually cold and dry. They lack zeal and vitality. They have gotten into the habit of foregoing daily prayer, abandoning personal daily Bible reading, ditching church and neglecting regular corporate worship. They have allowed superficial priorities to smother out spiritual ones. They have neglected the maintenance of their walk with God. As such, they have no reservoir of life or desire to draw from to share with unbelievers.

The New Testament has something to say to a Christian in this static position: "wake up from your slumber!" (Romans 13:11). And John quotes Jesus as he writes to the apathetic church in Sardis, saying, "Wake up! Strengthen what remains and is about to die, for I have not found your deeds complete in the sight of my God. Remember, therefore, what you have received and heard; obey it and repent" (Revelation 3:2-3). So don't be a comatose Christian!

Bad theology

One more reason some Christians don't aggressively evangelize the lost is because they have wrong thinking—they have tweaked theology. These people take biblical election to an unbalanced extreme. Their thinking goes like this: "The Bible teaches that God elected some for salvation before the foundation of the world. Only the elect will believe the gospel. Therefore we don't need to evangelize the lost because the non-elect will not believe the message, and because God is sovereign, He'll make sure the elect get saved anyway, apart from what I do."

Frankly, that kind of thinking is a lazy cop-out. God is sovereign and election is true. But that does not negate Jesus' command given to every

Christian when He said, "GO!"—to every creature...to the utter most part of the earth. May God awaken His Church everywhere to obey this call.

Questions for Review

1. Where in the Bible is the 'Great Commission' found?

_____

_____

_____

2. What is the main imperative in the 'Great Commission'?

_____

_____

_____

3. What was the 'Last Commission' Jesus gave to the church?

_____

_____

_____

4. Where does the word "witness" originally come from?

_____

_____

_____

5. What is an "ambassador"?

_____

_____

_____

6. How are you being an ambassador for Jesus?

_____

_____

_____

7. What does the word "gospel" mean?

_____

_____

_____

8. Give an example from the New Testament where it says one must believe in the resurrection of Jesus in order to be saved.

_____

_____

_____

9. Give an example where Jesus commanded unbelievers to repent in order to become believers.

_____

_____

_____

10. Write down a specific prayer of how you want God to help you become more faithful and active at sharing the gospel.

_____

_____

_____

_____

For further study on Go! **see these helpful resources:**
How to Give Away Your Faith, by Paul Little
Tell the Truth, by Will Metzger
Evangelism and the Sovereignty of God, by J. I. Packer
The Masterplan of Evangelism, by Robert E. Coleman
Evangelism Explosion, by D. James Kennedy
Nothing But the Truth, by John F. MacArthur
The Soul Winner, by Charles Haddon Spurgeon

8

Study!

"I have treasured the words of his mouth more than my daily bread."
(Job 23:12)

This chapter concerns the importance of personal Bible study in the life of every Christian. One commitment that every member of the church should make is the commitment to study (Ezra 7:10), remain in (John 15:5), memorize (Psalm 119:11), and meditate on (Psalm 119:48) God's Word. No habit you can form will have a greater overall impact on your life success than whether you commit to studying God's Word on a daily basis. God's will for every life is contained within the pages of the Bible. By studying it carefully in the power of the Holy Spirit you can grow like Jesus Christ to the glory of God the Father. Put another way, by carefully studying God's Word and then applying its principles to your life, you can live the victorious life God created you to live. James 1:25 says, "But the man who looks intently into the perfect law that gives freedom, and continues to do this...he will be blessed in what he does."

Why Study the Bible?

There are many good reasons to study the Bible. However, the best reason is that God commands it! In Colossians 3:16 Paul commands believers everywhere to "Let the word of Christ dwell in you richly." Like every command in Scripture, God's command to study the Bible is designed for your good. There are numerous benefits the Christian enjoys from studying the Bible. Here we examine four.

143

Encouragement

The first important benefit you gain from studying God's Word is *encouragement*. The Bible teaches (and we all know from first-hand experience) that life is full of trouble. Paul tells the Christians at Thessalonica that they should not be "unsettled" by trials because they are part of life (1 Thessalonians 3:3). He tells Timothy that "everyone who wants to live a godly life in Christ Jesus will be persecuted" (2 Timothy 3:12). Peter tells Christians everywhere not to be "surprised" when painful life events come (1 Peter 4:12). Jesus tells the disciples that because "no servant is greater than his master," they will experience persecution just like He did (John 15:20). To live in a fallen world is to experience many conflicts, struggles, and difficulties.

Because life is so full of trouble, it is very important to know where you can get timely encouragement. The Bible is the place! God's Word is literally jam-packed full of wonderful promises that offer encouragement when times are tough. For instance, in Philippians 4:19 Paul promises Christians that "God will meet all your needs according to his glorious riches in Christ Jesus." In Romans 8:38-39 Paul tells Christians that nothing can "separate" them from God's love as revealed in Jesus Christ. In John 14:27 Jesus promises His followers "peace" beyond what the world offers.

By immersing yourself in God's Word, you absorb truth that brings "comfort" (Psalm 119:52) and "hope" (Romans 15:4). The reason is that God's Word tells a story that ends in victory for every Jesus follower. Over and over again the psalmist calls God's law his "delight" (Psalm 119:24, 143). By studying the Word of God daily, you give God's Spirit opportunity to remind you of many bedrock truths like "Jesus is risen" (Matthew 28:6), Jesus reigns (Heb 8:1), and Jesus is coming again (Hebrews 9:28). When you reflect on these glorious truths in times of difficulty, you experience deep soul encouragement just like David who says: "The law of the LORD is perfect, reviving the soul" (Psalm 19:7).

Guidance

The second wonderful benefit the Christian gains from studying the Bible is *guidance*. Everybody needs reliable guidance. That is because life is full of difficult decisions. Teenagers must decide whom to befriend. College students must decide what to study. Graduates must decide which career to pursue. Young adults must decide whom to marry. Parents must decide how to raise their children. Working people must decide how to spend their time and money. None of these decisions is easy. Without reliable guidance, it is very easy to make the wrong choice. Making the wrong decision is especially easy when you are relying upon your own judgment, which the Bible says is frighteningly unreliable. Jeremiah 17:9 says, "The heart is deceitful above all things and beyond cure." Ecclesiastes 9:3 adds that people have "madness in their hearts" while they live.

Fortunately, the Bible contains counsel for every situation in life. There is no important matter in life that the Bible does not address. The Bible contains truth about relationships, marriage, conflict, money, parenting, work, citizenship, and even leisure! By prayerfully studying the Bible, you can receive God's guidance for every decision.

Protection

The third fantastic benefit the Christian enjoys from studying the Bible is *protection*. In particular, you enjoy protection from the devil's tricks. The Bible teaches very clearly that Christians have a fierce enemy called Satan, a "roaring lion" whose purpose is to "devour" God's people (1 Peter 5:8). Although many modern people, even many modern "religious" people deny his existence, the devil is real and deadly. Although the devil has been mortally wounded by Jesus' death on the cross and resurrection (Colossians 2:14-15), he remains a threat for believers until the day when he is finally destroyed once and for all at the end of history (Revelation 20:10).

Satan's primary tactic is deception. In John 8:44 Jesus calls him "the father of lies." Writing in the book of Revelation, the Apostle John calls Satan a deceiver (Revelation 20:10). Satan loves to fill the minds of believers and unbelievers alike with lies. Why? Because if he succeeds in convincing people that his lies are true, his job is done. Deceived people destroy themselves. Proverbs 10:21 says, "fools die for lack of judgment."

What are some of Satan's favorite lies? Here's one: It is normal and healthy to give full vent to your anger. Unfortunately, many people live like that lie is true. They express their anger with violent words and acts. The result is that they come to ruin. Naturally, the Bible predicts this result when it says, "A fool gives full vent to his anger" (Proverbs 29:11). Another of Satan's favorite lies is that marital infidelity is exciting and liberating. "Stolen water is sweet" (Proverbs 9:17), the devil purrs into the ear of the businessman traveling alone. Unfortunately, many people (men and women) live like that lie is true. They, too, come to ruin, discovering for themselves that in the end adultery is "bitter as gall," just as Proverbs 5:4 says.

Fortunately, you do not need to be waylaid by Satan's deceit. Rather, by studying God's Word and by meditating deeply upon its principles, you can protect yourself from Satan's lies and the self-destructive choices he wants you to make based on those lies. Make regular Bible reading your priority in life and discover for yourself the promise of Proverbs 2:11: "Discretion will protect you, and understanding will guard you."

Wisdom

The fourth great benefit the Christian gains by the faithful study of God's Word is *wisdom*. The more you know about God's ways, God's character, and God's priorities, all expressed in God's Word, the more wisdom you will gain. What is wisdom? Wisdom is simply the knowledge of how God's principles apply to life.

The world desperately needs wise men and women who can direct others in God's ways. Schools need wise principals who can order their schools according to God's truth. Nations need wise leaders who can make difficult decisions regarding foreign and domestic policy. Perhaps most of all, churches need wise pastors and elders who can help the body work together in accomplishing God's will for that church in the world. Unfortunately, truly wise men and women are rare, as the sorry state of many schools, nations, and churches makes clear.

Nevertheless, God's wisdom is for the taking. James 1:5 says, "If any of you lacks wisdom, he should ask God, who gives generously to all without finding fault, and it will be given to him." God's primary way of giving wisdom is through His Word. As Psalm 19:7 says, "The statutes of the LORD are trustworthy, making <u>wise</u> the simple." In 2 Timothy 3:15 Paul reminds his young friend how "the holy Scriptures...are able to make you <u>wise</u> for salvation through faith in Jesus Christ." Study Scripture diligently and grow wise. Not only will you bring "joy" to your family (Proverbs 10:1), but like many wise Christians who have gone before, you will "shine like the brightness of the heavens" (Daniel 12:3) to future generations.

How to Study the Bible

Now that we have explored *why* you should make study of the Bible a top priority in life, we turn to *how* you can study the Bible effectively. There are many good ways of studying the Bible and enjoying its benefits. The method that follows involves four steps: Yield, Observe, Distill, and Apply (YODA). We will start by discussing what it means to *Yield* to God's Word.

Yield

Yielding to Scripture means recognizing four of its key attributes. The first is its *perfection*.

Perfection

Listen to how the Old Testament describes the perfection of God's Word: "And the words of the LORD are flawless" (Psalm 12:6); "Righteous are you, O LORD, and your laws are right. The statutes you have laid down are righteous; they are fully trustworthy" (Psalm 119:137-138); "Your statutes are forever right" (Psalm 119:144); "you are near, O LORD, and all your commands are true" (Psalm 119:151); "Every word of God is flawless" (Proverbs 30:5).

The New Testament is equally insistent upon the utter perfection of God's Word. In 2 Timothy 3:16 Paul tells his young protégé Timothy that "All Scripture is God-breathed." In Matthew 5:18, the Lord Jesus Himself affirms the perfection of God's Word: "I tell you the truth, until heaven and earth disappear, not the smallest letter, not the least stroke of a pen, will by any means disappear from the Law until everything is accomplished."

What does it mean that God's Word is perfect? It means that every statement the Bible makes is true. First, every religious statement the Bible makes is true. When the Bible quotes Jesus saying, "I am the way and truth and the life. No one comes to the Father except through me" (John 14:6), you take that statement about salvation at face value. You conclude that outside of Jesus, "Salvation is found in no one else" (Acts 4:12).

However, the perfection of God's Word means even more than that every religious statement the Bible makes is true. You see, the Bible is true in *every* statement it makes, and not just religious statements. For instance, the perfection of God's Word means that when the Bible makes a statement about history, that historical statement is true. Moreover, when the Bible makes a statement about science, that scientific statement is true. Finally, when the Bible makes a statement about knowledge or about the nature of reality, that philosophical statement is true. Again, every word the Bible speaks is true. That is why Paul specifically tells Timothy that "All Scripture is God-breathed," as opposed to merely some of it (2 Timothy 3:16).

There are many people in the world today who deny the perfection of God's Word. Sadly, some of those people who deny the inerrancy of Scripture also claim to be orthodox Christians. However, be certain of this: Christian teachers who deny the absolute truth of every word of the Bible are teachers to avoid. Yielding to Scripture means having certainty in the perfection of God's Word.

Authority

Secondly, yielding to Scripture means recognizing its *authority*. Over and over again the psalmists recognize the authority of God's Word. At least twice the author of Psalm 119 says that he "trembles" before Scripture (Psalm 119:120, 161). That should be your attitude as well when you come before God's Word either in church or in your personal devotions. You should approach the Bible with awe, respect, and wonder, recognizing that it is God's authoritative message to humans in every age. The Bible teaches that God esteems the man or woman who approaches his Word in humble expectation: "This is the one I esteem: he who is humble and contrite in spirit, and trembles at my word" (Isaiah 66:2).

What else does accepting the authority of God's Word mean? It means trusting it more than your own judgment. Once again, human judgment is notoriously unreliable. Every day millions of people make choices that seem right to them at the time, but that in the end lead to destruction. Naturally, this is exactly what the Bible says: "There is a way that seems right to a man, but in the end it leads to death" (Proverbs 14:12).

The good news is that you do not need to be the victim of your own best (or perhaps worst!) judgment. Instead, by making the principles contained in God's Word your ultimate authority, you can preserve your life, avoid sin, bless your family, avoid Satan's snares, and most importantly, bring honor to God in the way you live. Decide now that God's Word will have absolute control of your life. Decide now that you will do what it says in every situation, even when doing so feels painful, which it will from time to time. Make Proverbs 3:5-6 your motto and your inspiration: "Trust in the LORD with all your heart and lean not on your own understanding; in all your ways acknowledge him, and he will make your paths straight."

Sufficiency

Thirdly, yielding to God's Word means recognizing its *sufficiency*. To recognize the sufficiency of Scripture means recognizing that it contains truth for each and every situation you face in life. Psalm 119:96 says: "To all perfection I see a limit; but your commands are boundless." By "boundless" the psalmist means that the wisdom contained in God's Word has no limits.

There are people in the world today who say that even though every statement in Scripture is true, the reach of Scripture is limited. In other words, Scripture does not speak to many important concerns of modern living. Critics like these argue that because of the time-bound nature of Scripture, people who want to live well must consult other sources of wisdom like modern psychology. You should reject any such claim.

The reality is that God's Word contains all the truth you need for victorious living. When Jesus prayed for the disciples before His arrest, He prayed: "Sanctify them by the truth, your word is truth" (John 17:17). Notice what He did NOT say: "Sanctify them by your truth, *and a good measure of Freudian analysis.*" Or, "sanctify them by your truth, *and multiple sessions of hypnotherapy.*" Like Jesus, Paul knew that Scripture was enough to make people whole. When Paul bid farewell to the Ephesian elders, he said: "Now I commit you...to the word of his grace, which can build you up" (Acts 20:32). Notice what he did NOT say: "Now I commit you to the word of his grace, *and to the wisdom of Carl Jung,* which can build you up." Again, God's Word contains all the truth we need for spiritual *and* emotional health.

None of this is to say that God can never use good Christian counselors, or even medication, to help struggling people. Rather, the point is that God's Word contains sufficient truth for life's problems. The goal of a Christian counselor should not be to introduce into the minds of clients ideas that are at odds with the Bible. Instead, the goal should be to lovingly, patiently, and carefully help people consider how the principles of God's Word bear on struggles of modern living, whether those struggles are anxiety, depression, conflict, temptation, or addiction.

The psalmist says that God's truth "last[s] forever" (Psalm 119:152). If God intends for His truth to last forever, it is a given that He intends for it to solve the problems of every age.

Power

Finally, yielding to God's Word means recognizing its *power*. There is nothing in the universe more powerful than the Word of God. When God speaks, amazing results follow. You exist, your family exists, the mountains exist, the seas exist, "the universe" (Hebrews 11:3) exists because God spoke them into reality. Contrary to modern scientific dogma, nothing existed before God spoke the world and its many wonders into being. Hebrews makes this clear when it says: "By faith we understand that the universe was formed at God's command, so that what is seen was not made out of what was visible" (Hebrews 11:3). Overcome with awe at the power of God to create the moon and the stars, the heavens and the angels from nothing, the psalmist declares: "Let them praise the name of the LORD, for he commanded and they were created" (Psalm 148:5).

The writers of Scripture use a number of metaphors to describe the power of God's Word. In Jeremiah 23:29, God likens his Word to "fire" and to a "hammer": " 'Is not my word like fire,' declares the LORD, 'and like a hammer that breaks a rock in pieces?' " Like fire, God's Word has the power to cleanse. Reading it carefully has the effect of burning away impurities in the mind and imagination. To read God's Word is to fill the mind with truth and beauty, leaving no place for evil thoughts. God's Word is also like a hammer in the power it contains to convict even the proudest heart. David, a strong and fierce warrior-king, was laid bare by God's Word spoken to him through the Prophet Nathan. Confronted with his sin of adultery and murder, David's defenses collapsed and he confessed: "I have sinned against the LORD" (2 Samuel 12:13).

The writer of Hebrews compares God's Word to a sword: "For the word of God is living and active. Sharper than any double-edged sword, it penetrates even to dividing soul and spirit, joints and marrow; it judges the thoughts and attitudes of the heart" (Hebrews 4:12). When you meditate deeply on God's Word you begin to see yourself clearly. Often what you see is not pretty. However, you cannot experience the joy of repentance if you do not know what is wrong in your life. By meditating on Scripture you give God's Spirit the opportunity to show you the areas of your life that need His correction. Once He makes you aware of those sins, you can repent and experience the joy of forgiveness.

Jesus uses the Word of God to withstand the devil. In Matthew 4 Satan tempts Jesus with fleshly gratification, human acclaim, and worldly power. Jesus resists each temptation by quoting Scripture. In response to Satan's fleshly temptation, Jesus says in verse 4: "It is written: 'Man does not live on bread alone, but on every word that comes from the mouth of God'." In response to Satan's temptation to human acclaim, Jesus says in verse 7: "It is also written: 'Do not put the Lord your God to the test'." And finally, in response to Satan's temptation to worldly power, Jesus says in verse 10: "Away from me, Satan! For it is written: 'Worship the Lord your God, and serve him only'." Jesus knew that nothing but the Word of God would enable Him to withstand the enemy's attacks. This should give you pause. If the Lord Jesus Himself needed the Word of God to resist Satan, we do too.

A practical way to yield

A practical way to yield to God's Word is to *pray* before you begin your Bible study. You might pray along these lines. First, thank God for the gift of His Word. Thank Him that through His Word He has allowed you to understand all you need for godly living. Thank Him that through his Word you can understand God's love, God's identity, God's revelation through Jesus Christ, God's plan for salvation, and God's priorities for the people who know Him. Thank Him for the benefits of encouragement, guidance, and protection that are yours when you faithfully study His Word.

Once you have thanked God for the *gift* of His Word, ask God to help you better *understand* His Word. Make your prayer that of the psalmist who prays, "Open my eyes that I may see wonderful things in your law" (Psalm 119:18). Follow his lead in praying for "discernment" (verse 125), and for "understanding" (verse 169).

You can make these requests with confidence for a number of reasons. First, as mentioned above, James 1:5 says that God gives wisdom in generous measure to those who ask Him in faith. By humbly asking God to help you better understand His Word, you are asking for wisdom. Proverbs 2:6 says, "For the Lord gives wisdom, and from his mouth come knowledge and understanding."

The second reason you can ask God confidently for understanding into His Word is that one of the Holy Spirit's activities is to help Christians understand the Bible. Listen to Paul describe the Holy Spirit's ministry of *illumination:* "We have not received the spirit of the world but the Spirit who is from God, that we may understand what God has freely given us" (1 Corinthians 2:12). God has freely given you His Word, and fully intends to help you understand its meaning for your life.

Observe

Once you have *yielded* by praying for God's help in understanding His perfect, authoritative, sufficient, and powerful Word, you are ready to begin step two in your personal Bible study. You are ready to *observe.* Observing the text involves six steps: *getting a journal, selecting a passage, surveying the field, reading the passage, asking questions, and writing a response.*

Get a journal

A necessary precursor to *observation* is acquiring a journal. Do not think that you need to buy anything fancy. In fact, a simple legal pad will do. On the other hand, if you are the type that enjoys writing in fine leather journals, then feel free to buy one for Bible study! The key is to have some kind of notebook in which you can keep your reflections. And in case you are tempted to skip acquiring a journal, know now that jotting down notes is an indispensable part of Bible study. In fact, you cannot effectively study the Bible without doing some writing. Moreover, keeping those notes in a permanent journal will be a great aid to you if God calls you to a teaching ministry.

Select a passage

The second preliminary step you must take before beginning to observe is obvious: *select a passage to study.* Here you really cannot go wrong. Paul says in 2 Timothy 3:16 that "All Scripture is...useful for teaching, rebuking, correcting and training in righteousness." Here Paul means just what he says. Every word of Scripture contains important spiritual nourishment for you. Moreover, if every word of Scripture is spiritually "useful" to you, it means that every word deserves your careful study.

On the other hand, that every word of Scripture is useful for spiritual growth does not mean that it is a good idea to select your passage for study randomly. For instance, if you are a new Christian and thus new to Bible study, it would probably not be good to begin Bible study in Leviticus or Jeremiah. This is not to suggest that those Old Testament books of the Law (Leviticus) and prophecy (Jeremiah) are unimportant. In fact, you will be missing out if you never study those books during your Christian career. It just means that some books of the Bible are more accessible to beginners than others.

If you are new to Bible study, then it would be great to begin with the Gospel of John. Like the other three Gospels (Matthew, Mark, and Luke), the Gospel of John tells the exciting story of Jesus' life on earth. In addition to many wonderful healings (Jesus heals a man born blind—John 9:1-34) and other amazing miracles (Jesus raises Lazarus from the dead—John 11:1-44), the Gospel of John has much to teach about the unique identity of Jesus Christ as the Son of God. Over and over again in John's Gospel, Jesus identifies Himself in the closest possible terms with the   Father: "I and the Father are one" (John 10:30); "I am in the Father and the Father is in me" (John 14:11); "He who hates me hates my Father as well" (John 15:23); "All that belongs to the Father is mine" (John 16:15).

In addition to having much to say about the identity of Jesus, the Gospel of John contains much about the vocation of Jesus. Jesus describes His messianic role in many important "I am" statements: "I am the bread of life" (John 6:35); "I am the light of the world" (John 8:12); "I am the gate" (John 10:9); "I am the way and the truth and the life" (John 14:6) "I am the true vine" (John 15:1); "I am the resurrection and the life" (John 11:25). A mature understanding of the person and ministry of Jesus requires a careful study of John.

Finally, the Gospel of John is a wonderful place to begin Bible study because it contains important truth about the identity of the Holy Spirit, or the "Comforter" as He is known throughout John, chapters 14-16. The Bible teaches that from day one of his Christian life, every reborn person is indwelt by the Holy Spirit (2 Corinthians 5:5). By studying the Gospel of John, you can gain a rich understanding of the function of the third member of Trinity in your life.

A second great book with which to begin Bible study is Paul's letter to the Philippians. Philippians is short, warm-hearted, and practical. Its four chapters are full of wonderful truth about how to live for Christ. Moreover, Philippians contains one of the most important passages in the entire Bible about Christian living: "Do nothing out of selfish ambition or vain conceit, but in humility consider others better than yourselves. Each of you should look not only to your own interests, but also to the interests of others. Your attitude should be the same as that of Christ Jesus" (Philippians 2:3-5).

On the other hand, if you already have a good grounding in the Bible, perhaps from having attended a good Bible church for a long time, there is no reason you cannot choose any section of Scripture for personal Bible study. For instance, you might choose to study the life of Joseph from Genesis 37-50. You might also choose to study the life of David as recorded in 1 and 2 Samuel. On the other hand, you could select one book from the Book of Psalms for careful study (the Psalms are made up of five books), or one of the Minor Prophets like Hosea. Again, you really cannot go wrong in making your selection. The important point is to select a passage and to jump in.

One more thought about passage selection. Remember, the Bible is a logical book. Better yet, it's an inspired collection of sixty-six logical books. Some of these books are narratives (Exodus, Ruth, 1 Kings, Mark, Acts, etc.). Others are theological treatises contained within personal letters (Romans, Colossians, 1 Peter, 1 John, etc.). Whatever the genre however, the ideas contained in every book are logically related. Not only are the passages within each book logically related, but the books themselves are logically related. In that sense, Scripture is like an epic novel.

Because Scripture is logical and tells a coherent story, your understanding of any particular text will be greatly enhanced if you understand that text in its context. That is why in personal Bible study you should avoid excessive jumping around. For instance, instead of selecting Hebrews 12 one day, Jeremiah 31 the next, and Revelation 20 the day after that, you would do far better studying Hebrews it its entirety before moving on to Jeremiah and Revelation. In short, although all Scripture is useful, you will get far more out of it by studying it in a systematic fashion. Keep the logical coherency of Scripture in mind when you select a passage for study on any particular day.

Once you have selected your passage for study (ten verses is a good amount), you are ready for your third step in observation. You are ready to *survey the field*.

Survey the field

What does it mean to *survey the field*? Simply put, it means taking in the big picture of your passage. As mentioned above, although the Bible contains many religious truths, it is far more than simply a catalogue of religious truths. Rather, the Bible tells a story—an epic story of God's redemption of man through the work of Jesus Christ. Every part of the Bible connects to that larger story.

When you survey the field you are really pausing to ask: "How does the Bible book I am studying fit within the Bible's grand story of God saving man?" For instance, Genesis explains how men and women went wrong in the first place. On the other hand, Revelation explains how this great story of God's salvation of the world through Jesus Christ will draw to a triumphant close.

In truth, surveying the field as a prelude to Bible study is not difficult. You can do it in ten minutes with the help of the right tool. The right tool is a study Bible, and there are many excellent ones like *The NET Bible*, *The MacArthur Study Bible*, *The NIV Study Bible*, *The Open Bible*, *The Life Application Bible*, just to name a few. By taking just a few minutes to read the introduction to the Bible book you are studying, you will grasp important background about the book that will make an enormous difference in your understanding of that book. That background could be historical information. For instance, a good introduction to the book of Daniel will explain the historical setting of the book: the Babylonian Exile. Moreover, that background could be the purpose of the letter. Any introduction to the book of Galatians will explain that Paul wrote that letter in response to a particular threat to the church. The point is this: by surveying the field of the passage you have chosen for study, you gain perspective which will allow the book to come into clear focus.

Read the passage

Now that you have surveyed the field of the passage you have selected for study, you are ready to *read the passage*. What should you know about reading Scripture?

First, you should read the text slowly. The Bible is full of meaning. If you rush through the step of reading your passage, you will miss important truth God has for you there. Read it with the same care and attention you would devote to a personal letter.

Secondly, you should read the text multiple times. Because Scripture is "living Word," you will discover that with each reading, different sections of your passage will jump out to you in different ways. It is not unusual to be struck by different sections of the passage in multiple careful readings.

Thirdly, you should read the text aloud. Revelation 1:3 says, "Blessed is the one who <u>reads</u> the words of [Scripture]...and blessed are the ones who <u>hear</u> it." For most of history, Christians never read Scripture themselves. Rather, they had Scripture read to them. They knew nothing of reading Scripture quietly to themselves, in the way people read novels. By verbalizing the Biblical text, you engage your ears and not just your eyes in the task of understanding the truth of the passage. Not only will you notice important details you would otherwise miss by reading aloud, but you will also be blessed by the artistry of the language of Scripture. You will discover that God's Word is true and beautiful! Finally, the importance of reading your passage out loud is another reason to pick a place for Bible study in which you have some privacy.

Having now *acquired a journal, selected a passage, surveyed the field,* and *read the passage,* you are ready to *ask questions.*

Ask Questions

Asking questions of your passage is at the heart of *observing.* You really have not begun to study Scripture until you have begun asking questions and writing down your thoughts. When you ask questions of the text you transition from casual observer to careful investigator. The Bible's richest blessings are reserved for those who investigate Scripture patiently and carefully, much like a detective. When you ask questions of the text rather than merely breezing through it in a careless fashion, you imitate the psalmist who "ponder[s]" God's Word (Psalm 119:95).

Although the following list is not comprehensive, here are some important questions to ask:

- What is the main subject of the passage?
- Why was the book written?
- Who is speaking?
- What is the key verse of the passage?
- What does the passage teach me about God's character?
- What does the passage teach me about God's will for His followers?
- What other passages in Scripture does this passage remind me of?

Write a response

Having now asked questions of the text, you are ready for the last and most important step in *observation*. You are ready to *write a response*. As mentioned above, an absolutely indispensable component of effective Bible study is writing responses to the questions you have posed. That is because writing about the text unlocks its meaning.

Here is a warning: in busy times you will be tempted to neglect this final step in *observation*. You will be tempted to short circuit observation by merely reading the text and not writing about it. However, you need to resist this temptation! Do not let the journal you acquired collect dust! If you remain faithful at writing even short responses, you will be amazed at the important insights God's Spirit gives you. On the other hand, if you fail to write, you will discover that an hour after finishing you may not remember what you studied.

Here's another warning: sometimes the passage you are studying will be immediately compelling for you. On those days it will be hard to stop writing. On other days, your passage may seem somewhat dull. Yet, even when your passage seems dry, force yourself to write something. If you do, you will find that even a passage that seems uninteresting at first blush will come alive to you as you reflect on it in writing.

Distill

Now that you have *asked questions* of your passage, and *written a response* in your journal, you are ready for step three. You are ready to *distill* the *observations* contained in your *written response* into "tools" for life. These spiritual tools should take the form of *promises* to rest upon, *principles* to remember, and *commands* to obey.

Here are some examples. Let us say that you are studying 1 Corinthians chapter 10. Verse 13 says this: "But when you are tempted, he will also provide a way out so that you can stand up under it." That passage can easily be *distilled* into a *promise* to rest upon. You might word that promise this way: "God promises to show me a way out of every temptation I face." Another possibility would be the following: "God promises to help me resist temptation by providing escape routes." How you distill your observations into promises is up to you. However, it is key that you do so, and that you write down the promise in your journal.

Hebrews 13:8 says: "Jesus Christ is the same yesterday and today and forever." You can easily distill this passage into a *principle* to remember. You might frame it this way: "Jesus never changes."

Finally, take Galatians 6:2. It reads: "Carry each other's burdens, and in this way you will fulfill the law of Christ." This verse can easily be distilled into a *command* to obey. You might word it this way: "Obey the law of Christ by sharing the troubles and problems of your friends."

This third step in your personal Bible study (*distill*) is very important. By forging your observations into simply written *promises* to rest upon, *principles* to remember, and *commands* to obey, you put the truth of God's Word into forms that you can remember. Moreover, God's Holy Spirit can then bring those truths to mind in situations where they apply. On the other hand, if you neglect to take the time necessary to distill your observations into promises, principles, and commands, you will very likely forget what you have learned, in which case your Bible study may be less valuable. Remember that the wonderful promise of James 1:25 is for those who study God's Word and then remember what it says: "But the man who looks intently into the perfect law that gives freedom, and continues to do this, not forgetting what he has heard, but doing it—he will be blessed in what he does."

Apply

After *yielding* to God's Word prayerfully (recognizing its perfection, authority, sufficiency, and power), then after *observing* your passage carefully (asking questions and writing responses), and finally after *distilling* your responses thoughtfully (forging them into memorable promises, principles, and commands), you are ready for the fourth and final step—you are ready to *apply* God's Word to your life.

This is the most exciting step, as well as the most perilous. Simply put, if you take step number four seriously and pattern your behavior on the truth of God's Word, you will be blessed. You will experience peace, security, and the special joy reserved for him who is an "instrument for noble purposes...prepared to do any good work" (2 Timothy 2:21). On the other hand, if you stop short of applying the truth that you have studied, even if you spend considerable time *thinking* about that truth, you will come to ruin. Jesus makes this stark reality plain in Matthew 7:24-25, which says:

> *Therefore everyone who hears these words of mine and puts them into practice is like a wise man who built his house on the rock. The rain came down, the streams rose, and the winds blew and beat against that house; yet it did not fall, because it had its foundation on the rock. But everyone who hears these words of mine and does not put them into practice is like a foolish man who built his house on sand. The rain came down, the streams rose, and the winds blew and beat against that house, and it fell with a great crash.*

Consider another passage about the importance of putting God's Word into practice. James 1:22-24 says:

> *Do not merely listen to the word, and so deceive yourselves. Do what it says. Anyone who listens to the word but does not do what it says is like a man who looks at his face in a mirror and, after looking at himself, goes away and immediately forgets what he looks like.*

James' point here is that Bible study is fruitless if you fail to act upon it. Acquiring Biblical knowledge for its own sake means very little if that knowledge does not translate into life change. God gave you His Word not so that you would be filled with knowledge (which "puffs up" according to 1 Corinthians 8:1), but so that you would be "thoroughly equipped for every good work" (2 Timothy 3:17). With His wonderful Word, God does not want to *fill* your brain half so much as He wants to *shape* your behavior.

This raises an important question: *how*, in practical terms, can you *apply* the truths of God's Word to your life? You can most effectively apply God's Word with careful planning. In other words, in the final minutes of your quiet time, take your calendar; note the appointments and activities you have that week; and then prayerfully decide how the promises, principles, and commands you have distilled in Bible study inform the way you will conduct yourself in those settings. If you take time for this careful planning, you will be amazed at how brilliantly the truths you have distilled dovetail with the challenges you anticipate that week.

Here is what that thoughtful planning might actually look like. Maybe the passage you are studying on a particular day is James 1:19-20: "My dear brothers, take note of this: Everyone should be quick to listen, slow to speak and slow to become angry, for man's anger does not bring about the righteous life that God desires." Let us then say that in your study time you distill your written responses on James 1:19-20 into the following *command*: "Say little, listen much, and be patient." An essential step in actually applying that command is to imagine (and then to write down in your journal!) how you intend to specifically obey that command this week in the circumstances you anticipate having. Therefore, you might write the following: "This week in my staff meeting, rather than blowing my top like I often do when my colleague disagrees with me, I will remember to 'say little, listen much, and be patient'." After praying for God's help in following through, you can set out with confidence saying along with Paul: "To this end I labor, struggling with all his energy, which so powerfully works in me" (Colossians 1:29).

When to Study the Bible

There is no hard and fast rule regarding *when* to study the Bible. The psalmist talks about meditating on God's promises "through the watches of the night" (Psalm 119:148). On the other hand, the Gospels say that it was Jesus' practice to meet with His Father "very early in the morning, while it was still dark" (Mark 1:35). If you are the type of person who wakes up cheerful, clear-minded, and early, it makes sense to set aside time in the morning for personal Bible study. By studying early you will protect against distractions later on. You will also enjoy having the whole day to experience the Holy Spirit guiding you through the promises, principles, and commands you meditated upon that morning. If, however, you are the type of person that cannot function before 10:00 a.m. and three cups of coffee, you certainly have the freedom to meet with God for study and prayer later in the day.

What is important about daily Bible study is not *when* you do it, but *that* you do it, and that you do it consistently. Pick a time morning, noon, or night when you feel fresh and then block it out on your calendar. Guard that time against all competitors. Bible study is like most endeavors in that it rewards those who approach it with discipline and consistency.

A Final Word of Encouragement

This chapter has discussed many important benefits enjoyed by the Christian who commits to daily, personal Bible study. However, there is one more benefit to mention. You see, in addition to gaining encouragement, guidance, protection, and wisdom, the man or woman who commits to studying God's Word as a top priority of life is rewarded with incredible wonder.

Wonder is essential for life. Without wonder life becomes tasteless and unendurable. The problem is that every worldly pleasure grows tiresome at some point. This is not because God's good gifts in the world are bad. Rather, it is because those gifts are finite and temporal, when as Solomon notes, the human heart aches for that which is infinite and eternal: "He has also set eternity in the hearts of men" (Ecclesiastes 3:11).

However, unlike the good but fleeting things of the world, the Word of God is both infinite and eternal. Scripture is infinite because it comes from the mind of a God of infinite wisdom. Scripture is eternal because it teaches that it will never pass away. Isaiah 40:8: "The grass withers and the flowers fall, but the word of our God stands forever."

Here is the good news. Because Scripture is both infinite and eternal, the study of Scripture is a pleasure that can never wane. It is a joy that can never grow stale. You will never come to a point when Scripture cannot challenge you, inspire you, and awe you. By making its exploration your highest priority, you dig in a mine of endless treasure.

Questions for Review

1. What is the main reason Christians should study the Bible? Give a verse to support your answer:

_____

_____

_____

_____

2. How does Bible study "encourage" the believer? Give examples:

_____

_____

_____

3. Can you think of a time in life when God used a particular Bible passage to guide you through a difficult situation? If so, describe the situation and the passage God used to direct you.

_____

_____

_____

4. What is Satan's primary tactic in attacking the Christian? How does regular Bible study guard against that?

_____

_____

_____

5. What does the "sufficiency of Scripture" refer to? Why is it essential for the Christian?

_____

_____

_____

6. What kind of power does biblical truth have? Give verses to support your answers:

_____

_____

_____

_____

7. What is the difference between Bible reading and Bible study? Why is it important to study the Bible, as opposed to merely reading it?

_____

_____

_____

8. Do you agree that effective Bible study requires writing a response? Why or why not?

_____

_____

_____

9. Are there any books of the Bible that you find particularly interesting and would like to study? List your top three and why you find them interesting.

_____

_____

_____

10. Do you currently have a time picked out for daily Bible study? If so, when is it? If not, what time do you believe would work best for you? Do you have someone to hold you accountable in this area?

_____

_____

_____

For further study on *Study!* **see these helpful resources:**
Encyclopedia of Bible Difficulties, by Gleason Archer
The New International Dictionary of the Bible, by J. D. Douglas
Evangelical Dictionary of the Bible, by Walter Elwell
The Moody Handbook of Theology, by Paul Enns
How to Read the Bible for all its Worth, by Gordon Fee & Douglas
   Stuart

Zondervan NIV Exhaustive Concordance, by Edward Goodrick
Living By the Book, by Howard Hendricks
How to Study the Bible for Yourself, by Tim LaHaye
Experiencing Pleasure and Profit in Bible Study, by D.L. Moody
Nelson's Complete Book of Bible Maps and Charts, by Thomas Nelson
The New Linguistic and Exegetical Key to the Greek New Testament, by
    Cleon L. Rogers
The Zondervan Pictorial Encyclopedia of the Bible, by Merrill Tenney
An Expository Dictionary of Biblical Words, by W. E. Vine
The Bible Knowledge Commentary (2 vol.), by John Walvoord & Roy Zuck
Talk Thru the Bible, by Bruce Wilkinson & Kenneth Boa

9

Pray!

"let everyone who is godly pray..."
(Psalm 32:6)

Prayer is hard work. Few people are masters at it. Most neglect it to one degree or another. Many Christians feel guilty about their apathetic prayer life. And many more believers would admit, if they were honest, that they do not enjoy praying. Yet, all Christians know that prayer should be a regular part of the Christian experience. So how can the average Christian make prayer a regular, fulfilling, vital discipline of everyday life? God has given the believer answers in His Word, the Bible, which is replete with examples of prayer and principles of prayer.

What is Prayer?

According to the Bible, prayer is talking to God. It is personal conversing and communing with the Creator of the universe. God talks to us through the Scriptures; we talk to God through prayer.

Prayer is either mentioned or modeled in almost every one of the sixty-six books of the Bible. All the great saints of the Bible prayed: Job (Job 42), Abraham (Genesis 18:22-33), Isaac (Genesis 26:25), Jacob (Genesis 32:9), Moses (Exodus 32:11), David (Psalm 51), Daniel (Daniel 9:4-19), Paul (Romans 1:9-10), John (Revelation 22:20), etc. When reading the prayers of these saints, we readily see that they were talking to a Person—the same way we would talk with an intimate relative or trusted friend.

Christian Prayer is Unique

Virtually every religion promotes praying to God. Almost everyone prays at one time or another. But biblical, Christian prayer is distinct from the prayer of every other religion. The Bible teaches that there is a right way to pray and a wrong way to pray. God does not listen to or answer every person's prayer. God says in Isaiah, "When you spread out your hands in prayer, I will hide My eyes from you; even if you offer many prayers, I will not listen" (1:15). And in Proverbs He warns, "If anyone turns a deaf ear to the law, even his prayers are detestable" (28:9). Jesus Himself said that the prayers of the Pagans were ineffectual (Matthew 6:7) and that the prayers of the religious hypocrites were worthless (Matthew 6:5). So if we want to please God and if we want our prayers answered, then we need to pray the right way.

Praying Like Jesus

Jesus is the model and the Master on true prayer. His disciples quickly discerned that in their day. They noticed that Jesus' prayer life was distinct, dynamic and sincere—very different from the prayers of the Pharisees and Sadducees—the legalistic, proud-hearted, self-appointed religionists of first century Israel.

One day early on in Jesus' ministry, one of His disciples approached Him after a time of prayer in solitude, and he requested of Jesus: "Lord, teach us to pray, just as John taught his disciples" (Luke 11:1). This was a bold request. And Jesus honored the request by showing His disciples how to pray.

This request tells us plainly that we need to be taught how to pray. True prayer does not come naturally or instinctively. Prayer is a supernatural and other-worldly engagement that transcends natural human abilities or inclinations. The natural man does not want to pray. That "which is born of flesh is flesh" (John 3:6, NASB). Natural man wants to trust in himself, not in God. To engage properly in the foreign, heavenly venture of direct communication with the God of the universe in prayer, we need to be taught. So Jesus taught His followers how to pray.

The prayer that Jesus taught His disciples is found in Matthew 6 and Luke 11. It is known as *The Our Father* or *The Lord's Prayer* and is the most famous prayer ever spoken. It is a simple prayer, containing merely forty words; and despite its simplicity it has been widely misunderstood, misinterpreted and abused. Nevertheless, it is the model that Jesus wanted all His believers of all times to follow. Gleaning its main points is imperative for the Christian. So we'll do just that, as we are guided by the context of the two respective chapters where the prayer was given.

Pray in private

Before Jesus gave the specific content of the prayer in Matthew 6:9-13, He mentioned other foundational principles for true prayer. The first one was His command for every believer to maintain a "private prayer life." He said, "When you pray, go into your room, close the door and pray to your Father, who is unseen" (6:6). Here's the first secret to having regular success in prayer—you need to deliberately sequester yourself to be alone with God. If you don't make a priority of formally isolating yourself to meet with God, then the activities, business and distractions of the world will squelch and inhibit your prayer life.

This was not just an idealistic suggestion that Jesus was giving. Isolation is a practical necessity for vital prayer. Jesus prayed this way routinely. It was a discipline and habit of His life. Mark 1:35 says this about Jesus' prayer life: "Very early in the morning, while it was still dark, Jesus got up, left the house and went off to a solitary place, where he prayed." If we want to pray like Jesus, then we need to cultivate the habit of getting alone with God.

But in this day and age, countless people will argue, "I can't pray like that—that's unrealistic—I'm too busy...I can't ever be alone... my kids won't allow it...my job requires too many hours." Excuses, excuses. It's just a matter of priorities. Do what Jesus did—get up very early. It's a sacrifice. We make sacrifices for lesser things all the time. We need to be heavenly-minded and stop being so earthly-minded all the time. Prayer is hard work; prayer is a struggle. But it's worth it.

Daniel knew the importance of private prayer. He prayed in his room alone, on his knees, every day—three times a day (Daniel 6:10). And it almost cost him his life. That is sacrifice. It is said that Susanna Wesley, that godly woman of the 1700's, isolated herself for prayer away from her sixteen-plus children, by covering herself under a blanket so she could have some privacy with God!

My mother-in-law is a woman of prayer. For thirty years she has made a daily habit of finding quiet time with God for prayer. She'll do whatever is necessary to talk with the Father alone—get up while it's still dark; wait til the last person has gone to sleep and then begin prayer. I have even seen her sneak out into the garage and hide in the van early in the morning to pray where she would not disturb others and also so she could be alone with God in private—just as Jesus commanded. Do whatever it takes!

Pray with your mind

The next foundational principle of prayer Jesus gave was the command not to "babble like the pagans" (Matthew 6:7). Before telling us how to pray, He told us how not to pray. Here Jesus was decrying the most common kind of prayer that is practiced the world over, in His day and even in our day. It's the common practice of praying a *mantra*. It is characterized by rote memorization and repetition of a word, phrase, or many phrases, over and over and over. In Hinduism, practitioners will recite the name of a Hindu god, like "*Om*," incessantly until they manage to tire out the deity, and hence force the deity to do one's will.

This is not prayer, but meaningless repetition. Jesus condemned this practice, for it was an insult to God. He will not be wheedled, cajoled, or manipulated like a marionette from the wooing of countless words. Those who pray with "*mantras*" do so because they think they will "be heard because of their many words" (Matthew 6:7). But Jesus said, "Do not be like them, for your Father knows what you need before you ask Him" (6:8).

Despite Jesus' caution to not engage in rote memorization and meaningless repetition during prayer, many so-called Christians and churches have incorporated this very practice. Countless "Christians" recite the Lord's Prayer itself like it is some magical incantation, repeating it over and over, in the hopes of getting God to move.

One of the dangers of engaging in rote memorization of a prayer, is that the prayer will quickly lose its meaning. Rote repetition quickly becomes a thoughtless, mindless, routine activity—simply going through the motions without any conviction regarding the meaning of the words.

A perfect example of this is the fact that many practicing Muslims today memorize the *Koran* in Arabic, and repeat it over and over. Yet many of those who have it memorized and recite it don't even understand Arabic—they don't know what they are saying. There is no comprehension. Yet they think their god hears them by virtue of their many words. This was the kind of prayer Jesus was condemning.

Biblical prayer, on the other hand, was first and foremost to be personal, understandable words of communication directed toward an intelligible God who communicates with His people in comprehensible language. Paul said Christian prayer was to be typified with understandable language and comprehension. "Unless you speak intelligible words with your tongue, how will anyone know what you are saying? You will just be speaking into the air....I will pray with my spirit, but I will also pray with my mind; I will sing with my spirit, but I will also sing with my mind" (1 Corinthians 14:9, 15).

Jesus' Principles of Prayer

After establishing the preliminaries of true prayer, Jesus then told His disciples, "This, then, is how you should pray" (Matthew 6:9). What follows is the content of the *Lord's Prayer*. The prayer Jesus gave them was intended to be a paradigm for prayer, not a canned liturgical script to be memorized and muttered incessantly. He was showing them "how" to pray more than "what" to pray. He was demonstrating a model for prayer, not a *mantra* of prayer. The *Lord's Prayer* is a divine outline of how to directly communicate with the God of the universe. Jesus was giving parameters and principles of true biblical prayer, not a prescriptive mandate for rote recitation.

Jesus' model prayer begins with an invocation and then includes six petitions. Jesus intended His followers to use this framework when talking to God. Let's consider Jesus' principles of prayer found in the *Lords' Prayer*.

Prayer should be God-centered

Jesus taught His disciples that prayer needs to be God-centered, for Jesus began His prayer by saying, "Our Father in heaven, hallowed be your name" (Matthew 6:9). Prayer needs to begin with a conscious recognition of who God is—and here Jesus tells us that God is a Father and that God is holy.

Prayer is first and foremost the verbal declaration and acknowledgment that God is worthy of worship, glory, honor, praise and adoration. We need to begin our prayers by telling Him so. He needs to be revered, feared, respected and highly esteemed. That is what "hallowed" means.

There is no room for approaching God with a disrespectful familiarity, or the casual irreverence that seems to be gaining popularity these days. Too many refer to the transcendent God with the loathsome refrain, "the man upstairs." I was recently given a free book on prayer. The very first page refers to God as an "old man." I didn't need to go on to page two. The Bible says pointedly that "God is not a man" (Numbers 23:19). Too many have forgotten that God required Moses to remove his sandals before approaching Him, for He is Holy! And when we talk to Him, we need to treat Him accordingly.

Giving God preeminence and proper reverence in prayer has been the pattern of all the saints throughout biblical history. Moses begins his long prayer of thanksgiving after the Exodus by first speaking of how great God is, jubilantly declaring, "The LORD is a warrior" (Exodus 15:3). Hannah starts her memorable prayer by saying "There is no one holy like the LORD" (1 Samuel 2:2). Solomon begins his extended dedicatory prayer by saying, "O LORD, God of Israel, there is no God like you" (1 Kings 8:23). David begins his prayer of deliverance by singing, "The LORD is my rock, my fortress and my deliverer" (Psalm 18:2). Isaiah begins his prayer of praise by adoring God: "O LORD, you are my God...you have done marvelous things" (25:1). Daniel was exemplary in this manner, for his great prayer of supplication begins this way: "O LORD, the great and awesome God, who keeps his covenant of love with all who love him and obey his commands" (9:4). And Nehemiah begins his memorable prayer lauding God by saying, "LORD God of heaven, O great and awesome God" (1:5).

The lesson here for us is to get our eyes off ourselves when it comes to prayer. It's all too common to go to prayer and immediately begin by demanding, "Gimme, gimme, gimme!" Prayer is a time for worshipping God, not for being a leech (Proverbs 30:15). God is not a magic genie in a bottle who is there just to grant our self-centered wishes. So when you go to prayer, begin by mimicking the angels of Revelation who pray to God saying, "Holy, holy, holy is the Lord God Almighty" (4:8).

Pray according to God's will

The next principle of prayer after focusing on *who* God is, is to focus on *what* God wants. Jesus tells His disciples to pray, "your kingdom come, your will be done" (6:10). Jesus is saying that when we pray, we first and foremost should be concerned with what God wants—His will, not ours. Jesus Himself prayed with this submissive mindset just before His arrest in the Garden of Gethsemane the night before He was crucified. He knew His torture, humiliation and death were imminent, but nevertheless He said to the Father in prayer, "Father...not my will, but yours be done" (Luke 22:42).

Prayer is seeking after God's will and direction—trying to discern the very mind of God. It is a personal quest to obtain supernatural wisdom from heaven so that we can use that wisdom to amend our short-sighted, fallen, sinful, self-centered tendencies. Prayer is not primarily about telling God what He should do for us. It's not our will that matters, but His.

This concept of humility and selflessness in prayer is actually quite foreign in many quarters of Christian churches today. At least in many American churches, the goal of prayer is to squeeze God for all He's got—and to squeeze hard. Many so-called preachers and teachers are telling their people to "demand" things from God in prayer. The emphasis is on material possessions and wealth. And, supposedly, the more you demand, the more it is a sign that you have "great faith," for God wants us to be *bold* in prayer. They tell us we need to come to Him with confidence and expect health, wealth and earthly prosperity!

The truth is that this mindset is unabashed hedonism. It is totally antithetical to the true prayers of the Bible. In the parable of the Pharisee and the tax collector, Jesus condemned the religious Pharisee for his self-centered, pompous prayer that focused on earthly things. Jesus commended the tax collector for his prayer that was selfless, God-centered and devoid of any self-indulgent pursuit of pleasure or "things" (Luke 18). Jesus condemned the practice of having a fixation on earthly "things." He said,

> *Do not store up for yourselves treasures on earth, where moth and rust destroy, and where thieves break in and steal. But store up for yourselves treasures in heaven, where moth and*

rust do not destroy, and where thieves do not break in and steal. For where your treasure is, there your heart will be also (Matthew 6:19-21).

So when you go to prayer, after first praising God for who He is, then seek what He wants. Praying according to God's will is a teaching replete in the New Testament. But one other passage stands out regarding this truth—1 John 5:14-15. It says,

> *This is the confidence we have in approaching God: that if we ask anything according to his will, he hears us. And if we know that he hears us—whatever we ask—we know that we have what we asked of him.*

This is an amazing verse with a tremendous promise for the believer. God tells us we can be totally confident in our prayer life. But this verse does not say that we can have whatever we want. God will only grant what we ask that is in keeping with His will. So there are limits and parameters on what we can pray for. We need to pray for God's will, not ours.

God does not answer all prayers. Nor does He honor a prayer just because it was prayed sincerely. Many prayers are sincerely wrong. We need to pray according to truth. We need to pray things that are consistent with God's revealed written revelation found in the Bible. That's praying according to His will.

I will never forget the time when I was in college at a student-run vespers service held on a Sunday evening. The leadership team of about ten students met for prayer prior to the start of the service. One of the leaders prayed a prayer something like this: "Dear Father, we ask that you soften Satan's heart and bring him to repentance so that he might give up his evil ways and be saved." Everyone else in the group was speechless when they heard the sincere and unprecedented request.

The student who said the prayer was a sweet, sincere believer with a compassionate heart—which is admirable. But his prayer was not in God's will and God is not going to answer it. God has already revealed His will about Satan, the Devil. Satan will never repent. He will just get worse as time goes on. And his fate is in eternal hell, the lake of fire which was created by God to punish him and his evil angels (John 8:44; Matthew 10:28; 25:41; Revelation 20:7-10).

You cannot be ignorant if you want to pray according to God's will. Your prayers need to coincide with truth as God has revealed it in the Bible. Hence, this is another reason why you need to be taught how to pray. Just as you need to teach your children how to pray, who will frequently say, "Dear God, save everyone in the whole world." God is grieved over those who won't be saved (Ezekiel 18:32), but He has clearly told us that everyone won't be saved, for some people love their sin more than they love God, Jesus or heaven (John 1:11; 3:19).

Pray with a dependent attitude

After first acknowledging the greatness of who God is and what God wants, then Jesus says to pray with a spirit of dependence in our requests. He says, "Give us today our daily bread" (Matthew 6:11). "Daily bread" refers to our basic necessities in life—food, clothing, shelter. Jesus is reminding the believers that everything we need in life comes from God in heaven. Just as the book of James says, "Every good and perfect gift is from above, coming down from the Father of the heavenly lights" (1:17). Paul affirms this truth as well when he asks, "What do you have that you did not receive?" (1 Corinthians 4:7). In other words, he was reminding the Christian that everything you do have you received as a gift from God.

In a way Jesus was telling His disciples that they were spiritual paupers—we come to God as needy beggars, dependent on His grace, love, mercy and riches for everything in life. To admit this is to be humble. Such a humble attitude flies in the face of today's American credo—the self-sufficient attitude of rugged individualism, that says, "You can do or get whatever you desire if you want it bad enough and work hard enough." Or the equally fallacious refrain that says, "God helps those who help themselves." That is not a biblical thought. That is a humanistic concept. We can't help ourselves—we are helpless. King David knew this; he prayed, "we are dust" (Psalm 103:14). Jesus said to His disciples, "apart from Me you can do *nothing*" (John 15:5)!

With this petition Jesus was also instructing His followers to be thankful. All of our prayers should be seasoned with deliberate and specific gratitude for what God has provided. Not only should we ask God for our daily provisions, but we should thank Him each time He provides. In the Gospel accounts, every time Jesus is about to eat something He first thanks God the Father for the provision...every time (Matthew 14:19; 15:36; 26:26; 26:27). We should do the same. Do you thank God for every meal you eat—breakfast, lunch and dinner—no matter where you are? Psalm 69:30 says, "glorify Him with thanksgiving." Paul commands Christians everywhere to "give thanks in all circumstances, for this is God's will" (1 Thessalonians 5:18).

In the parallel passage of Luke it says, "Give us each day our daily bread" (11:3). There is an emphasis on the reality of praying "daily." Earlier Jesus said that we should have a formal, private prayer time with God—here He adds that it needs to be a daily discipline. Do you pray every day? Do you set aside a specific time each day to formally commune with the Father? We should. A healthy, mature, dynamic Christian life is built on the foundation of a quality, committed, formal disciplined time of quiet prayer with God.

I do a lot of counseling. Whenever a Christian couple meets with me to fix their problems, one of the first questions I always ask is, "What is your devotional life like? Tell me about your walk with God. Describe your individual daily prayer life." The overwhelming majority of the time what I hear is, "Well we really don't pray together that much." Or those who are really honest usually admit, "I can't remember the last time we prayed together as a couple." I think, "No wonder your marriage is falling apart! You're trying to live life in your own strength." We can't live life successfully on our own in any area. We need to depend upon God for everything, and we manifest that dependence by praying to Him every day, saying, "Dear God, please give us this day what we need today to survive."

So pray every day, asking God to provide the basics for life, and thank Him every time He provides.

Confess your sins to God

After petitioning God for the basic provisions in life Jesus tells His disciples to confess their sins: "Forgive us our debts, as we also have forgiven our debtors" (Matthew 6:12). Luke 11:4 says forgive us our "sins." In Luke the word for sins is *hamartia*, from which we get "hamartiology" which is the study of the doctrine of sin. Matthew uses the word "debt" as a metaphorical expression to show that our sin is an offense toward God and a violation of His holy law which we have transgressed. As such, we are indebted to Him and deserving of a penalty. We need His forgiveness because of our sin.

Here Jesus is clearly telling believers that they need to do regular spiritual inventory and maintenance regarding the ongoing battle with sin. Recently I have come across a false teaching that is gaining popularity in the Evangelical church. It is the idea that says since all of a person's sins were forgiven by God at the moment of justification (when a person is born again), then there is no need for a Christian to confess his or her sins to God after getting saved. "Why do I need to keep confessing my sins to God when He has already forgiven all of my sins—past present and future—when I was born again?" I have had well-meaning Christians tell me that repeatedly. This is a growing problem—and a serious one.

It is true that at the moment of justification or true conversion (when one puts personal faith in Christ and His gospel) that God declares the sinner totally righteous ("Not guilty!), and He sees the sinner as He does Christ. But we still have sin living inside of us (Rom 7:14-25; 1 Jn 1:8). And it will be with us until we die or until Christ comes to glorify our human bodies. In the meantime, we will battle with sin and give in to sin. So we need to regularly confess our acts and thoughts of sin to God. This is what John meant when he wrote, "If we confess our sins, He is faithful and just and will forgive us our sins and purify us from all unrighteousness" (1 John 1:9).

Daily confessing your sins to God does not impugn the work of Christ's sacrifice on the cross in any way, nor does it imply that we can lose our salvation or that all of our sins are not forgiven. Rather, it has to do with maintaining a healthy fellowship and communion with God on a personal level as one of His children. For instance, when my child does something wrong or disobedient, he has sinned against me. As the parent, I still love him unconditionally and he is still part of the family. But the act of disobedience has strained the relationship. But then the child is convicted, apologizes, asks for forgiveness and our fellowship is restored once again on a personal and practical level.

That is how it is with God. We need to keep a clean slate with Him regarding our daily living by regularly confessing our sins and asking for His forgiveness. Every Christian should have an ongoing "confessional" life. Paul told the Corinthian Christians to examine themselves before

God (1 Corinthians 11:28). James commanded Christians to confess their sins to God. He wrote,

> *Wash your hands, you sinners, and purify your hearts, you double-minded. Grieve, mourn and wail. Change your laughter to mourning and your joy to gloom. Humble yourselves before the Lord, and he will lift you up (4:8-10).*

In the last chapter of his epistle he commands Christians plainly: "confess your sins" (5:16). Nothing could be clearer. Christians need to confess their sins to God daily in prayer, just as Jesus said.

In addition to confessing our ongoing sins, we need to ask God to help us forgive others: "Forgive us our debts, as we forgive our debtors." We cannot forgive other people in our own strength. True forgiveness is a supernatural transaction. So we need to ask God for help.

Forgiving others takes supernatural love. And God has imparted divine love to the Christian. Romans says that "God has poured out his love into our hearts by the Holy Spirit" (5:5). Therefore all Christians have the capacity to forgive those who sin against them. There is no excuse for a Christian to withhold forgiveness toward others by coddling a grudge. But the sad reality is that many a Christian has been sapped of joy and has been spiritually crippled by harboring unforgiveness toward others.

Prolonged unforgiveness gives birth to the root of bitterness which spawns unmitigated devastation and interpersonal dysfunction (Hebrews 12:15; Galatians 5:15). Christian marriages have been shipwrecked through divorce because of simple unforgiveness.

The Bible says, "don't let the sun go down on your anger" (Ephesians 4:26). That means you need to keep on forgiving—every day—no matter how many times someone sins against you. There is no one who has sinned against you more than you have sinned against God. Yet, if you are a Christian God still forgives all your sins. He does not hold a grudge against you for something you did to hurt Him seventeen years ago. Thankfully He remembers our sins no more (Isaiah 43:25). If we could only do the same toward others as Jesus commanded us.

Pray for spiritual deliverance

Jesus concludes the *Lord's Prayer* by telling His disciples to pray for spiritual deliverance: "And lead us not into temptation, but deliver us from the evil one" (Matthew 6:13). This request is preventative in nature. Jesus is telling believers they need to think ahead. They need to safeguard their spiritual welfare by systematically building up their defenses, appropriating all that God has promised to supply by way of protection and provision. Jesus is reminding the believer that life is a spiritual war and the enemy is relentlessly on the attack. We cannot be spiritually negligent or nonchalant.

Jesus refers here to the "evil one." He is talking about the devil, Satan. Satan is a real being. He is supernatural, powerful, totally evil and needs to be taken seriously. The Bible says he is a vicious "roaring lion, seeking someone to devour" (1 Peter 5:8). He is the god of this evil world system (2 Corinthians 4:4) whose specialty is moral, religious and spiritual deception. He is prolific at distorting the truth.

Regular, vigilant prayer is the greatest defense against the wiles of the devil. Paul said,

> Put on the full armor of God so that you can take your stand against the devil's schemes. For our struggle is not against flesh and blood, but against the rulers, against the authorities, against the powers of this dark world and against the spiritual forces of evil in the heavenly realms. Therefore put on the full armor of God, so that when the evil day comes, you may be able to stand your ground...**pray** in the Spirit on all occasions with all kinds of **prayers** and **requests**. With this in mind, be alert and always keep on **praying** for all the saints (Ephesians 6:11-13, 18).

Paul's clarion call to prayer against the devil echoes the words of Jesus. We will fail repeatedly in our Christian life if we neglect praying for God's protection against the devil.

When we sin it is not the devil's fault. But the devil can entice us into temptation and sin if we are unprepared, naïve and ignorant. God promises to give us supernatural wisdom for living if we would just ask in faith (James 1:5). Part of that wisdom we ask for needs to be related to how we can best avoid the devil's hidden snares of sinful temptation that confront us daily. So in your regular private times of prayer with God, ask for specific deliverance from incidents of satanic temptation. Follow the example of Jesus who prayed for Peter's spiritual deliverance from the devil:

> *Simon, Simon, Satan has asked to sift you as wheat. But I have prayed for you, Simon, that your faith not fail. And when you have turned back, strengthen your brothers (Luke 22:31-32).*

Conclusion

So much more could be said about prayer. But following Jesus' pattern of prayer in Matthew 6 and Luke 11 is the place to begin. Take His words to heart and begin to develop a habit of prayer. Start small if prayer is not yet a daily routine in your life. Make a goal of spending the first ten or fifteen minutes of your day with God. You will quickly discover that God will meet with you personally in prayer and the sweet fellowship you have with Him will eventually become a joy, desire, and practice you can't live without.

Questions for Review
1. What is prayer?

_____

_____

_____

2. Give two references of where the *Lord's Prayer* is given in the New Testament

_____

_____

_____

3. What are the two preliminary truths about prayer that Jesus gives before He says the *Lord's Prayer*?

_____

_____

4. How is Biblical prayer different than Hindu meditation?

_____

_____

_____

5. How can Jesus' prayer life be a model for our own? (see Mark 1:35)

_____

_____

_____

6. Did you pray in private for an extended period of time today?

_____

_____

_____

7. Describe your current prayer life. a.) Do you have a routine? b.) Do you pray every day? c.) When was the last time you had quality prayer time alone? d.) If you are married, do you pray with your spouse? e.) When was the last time you prayed with your spouse? f.) Do you pray with your children? g.) How often?

_____

_____

_____

8. Who can hold you accountable to maintain a daily prayer time?

_____

_____

_____

9. What are the most pressing issues in your life right now? Write those down then commit them to God in prayer:

_____

_____

_____

_____

10. Write down the ways God has blessed you or answered prayer in the last seven days and then thank Him specifically for being gracious and kind to you; tell God how awesome He is by reflecting on His character and His attributes:

_____

_____

_____

_____

_____

_____

_____

_____

_____

_____

_____

_____

_____

_____

_____

_____

For further study on *Pray!* see these helpful resources:
The Complete Works of E. M. Bounds on Prayer, by E. M. Bounds
A Call to Spiritual Reformation, by D. A. Carson
The Jesus Habits, by Jay Dennis
The Hour that Changes the World, by Dick Eastman
A Woman's Call to Prayer, by Elizabeth George
The Prayer of Jesus, by Hank Hanegraaff
Prayer, The Great Adventure, by David Jeremiah
All the Prayers of the Bible, by Herbert Lockyer
Seeking God, by Richard Mayhue
Prevailing Prayer, by D. L. Moody
With Christ in the School of Prayer, by Andrew Murray
The Power of a Praying Wife, by Stormie Omartian
The Prayers of Christ, by C. H. Spurgeon
The Power of Prayer in a Christian's Life, by C. H. Spurgeon
Classic Sermons on Prayer, by Warren Wiersbe

10

Think!

"take captive every thought
to make it obedient to Christ"
(2 Corinthians 10:5)

Christianity is distinct from every other religion in the world in that it puts a premium on thinking. Biblical Christianity is a faith about objective truth, a supremely logical, orderly and consistent God, a Savior who called Himself "the truth" (John 14:6), and written Scriptures whose veracity is based upon its self-proclaimed inerrancy. The believer is said to have the "mind" of Christ (1 Corinthians 2:16), the thoughts of the Holy Spirit (1 Corinthians 2:10), and is expected to reason on a heavenly, supernatural level in assessing true reality (Colossians 3:2).

True religion is not about feelings, sentiment, popular opinion, or personal preference. True religion is about right thinking based on objective, knowable, unchanging, eternal truth.

We can Know Truth...Really!

We live in a day where postmodernism reigns supreme in the realm of ideas and how people think. It is an esoteric and confusing worldview that means a lot of different things to a lot of different people. But one common theme that stands out about postmodern thought is the notion that all truth is relative, or that ultimate truth cannot truly be known with any confidence or certainty. To say the least, it's quite a depressing and pessimistic worldview.

Christianity is the polar opposite of such a hopeless view. The Bible dogmatically affirms that there is truth, that truth is objective, universal, and knowable. Take for example the following Scriptures that speak with clarion boldness that we can know truth:

> *I know that my Redeemer lives, and that in the end he will stand upon the earth (Job 19:25).*

> *I know that the LORD saves his anointed, he answers him from his holy heaven (Psalm 20:6).*

> *Know that the LORD is God. It is he who made us and we are his (Psalm 100:3).*

> *I know, O LORD, that your laws are righteous (Psalm 119:75) I know that the LORD is great, that our Lord is greater than all gods (Psalm 135:5).*

> *I am the good shepherd; I know my sheep and my sheep know me—just as the Father knows me and I know the Father—and I lay down my life for the sheep (John 10:14-15).*

> *I know whom I have believed, and am convinced that he is able to guard what I have entrusted to him for that day (2 Timothy 1:12).*

> *We know that we have come to know him if we obey his commands (1 John 2:3).*

> *I write these things to you who believe in the name of the Son of God so that you may know that you have eternal life (1 John 5:13).*

So the Bible says we can know many things with certainty. We can know that God is alive, that He answers prayer, that He is a great God and the only God. We can know that His Word is true and trustworthy. We can know that we know Him. And we can even know, with absolute confidence right now, that we have eternal life! Only biblical Christianity makes that claim. So much for postmodern skepticism.

This is a breath of fresh air. Being able to know truth with unshakable confidence provides great freedom, stability, joy and peace of mind. Because of this unique approach to reality, the Christian can live life with security, enthusiasm and a rare exuberance.

God Cares about how We Think

According to the Bible, how we live depends on how we think and what we think. Our faith flows from our ability to reason and accurately comprehend spiritual truth. In Christianity, behavior follows knowledge; duty flows from doctrine; practice comes from precepts. Conduct results from content. This means that if we want to live right, first we have to think right.

According to Paul

This truth was basic for the Apostle Paul. There is an evident pattern to the way he writes his epistles in keeping with this truth. In Ephesians, for example, Paul first gives three chapters of truth, indicatives, and principles of Christian living, primarily addressing the mind and how we should think. Then he follows with three practical chapters of how we should live and how to apply those truths. For Paul, it was plain that we cannot be expected to live the right way until we first think the right way.

That's why he labors to teach doctrine first, then he gives commands for living based on that doctrine. Paul cared about how Christians thought. He knew God wanted control of their minds first, then right behavior would follow suit.

This pattern is most evident in Paul's lengthy epistle to the Romans. In the first eleven chapters Paul gives comprehensive teaching, biblical principles and theological truth on the basic doctrines of the Christian faith. It is not until chapter twelve that he finally begins exhorting Christians how to live. The first eleven chapters tell Christians how to think. In chapter twelve Paul begins giving a flurry of imperatives on right behavior. In the first eleven chapters there are practically no commands, but in chapter twelve alone Paul gives more than thirty. Paul knew you can't live right until you think right.

I remember once when a fellow pastor boasted to me that he "did not waste time teaching people doctrine; instead I just tell them to love Jesus." That sounds spiritual, but that statement is fatally flawed. The goal is to love Jesus, but we can't love Jesus until we know who Jesus is and what biblical love is. Right thinking on love comes first.

"Doctrine" is not a dirty word. It's actually a biblical word (Titus 2:1). It simply means "teaching" and in the New Testament it refers to supernatural revelation that God has given to us so that we might know Him better. Everything true there is to know about Jesus comes from the "teaching" or "doctrine" of the Bible, primarily the New Testament. It is not possible to love Jesus apart from knowing biblical doctrine about Him. So in order to correctly know Jesus, love Jesus and serve Jesus, we must first comprehend biblical "doctrine" about Him. Right thinking precedes right behavior and devotion to Christ.

That's why Paul gave this beautiful balance about living the Christian life: "Watch your life and your doctrine closely" (1 Timothy 4:16). Right behavior cannot be dichotomized from right doctrine. They are inextricably bound together.

According to Jesus

Jesus commanded believers to love God "with all your mind" (Matthew 22:37; cf. Mark 12:33). The word for "mind" here literally means "understanding, intelligence, the faculty of comprehension." It has to do with how we think. Loving God is an act of worship. So Jesus said we are to worship God with our minds; cautious, careful, holy thinking is an act of devotion to God.

Jesus taught further on this issue when He declared that our behavior is dictated by our thinking. What we say and what we do is a result of what is going on in the inner recesses of our being.

> For out of the overflow of the heart the mouth speaks. The good man brings good things out of the good stored up in him, and the evil man brings evil things out of the evil stored up in

*him (Matthew 12:34-35). But the things that come out of the
mouth come from the heart, and these make a man 'unclean.'
For out of the heart come evil thoughts, murder, adultery, sexual
immorality, theft, false testimony, slander (Matthew 15:18-19).*

In these verses the word "heart" refers to the rational, self-conscious part of a person, including the will, desires and mind. So Jesus was simply saying that our actions flow from our thinking.

This is in keeping with the Old Testament which taught that the heart was command-central of the inner person. Consider Proverbs 4:23, which warns, "Above all else, guard your heart, for it is the wellspring of life." In other words, the Bible says to make a priority of protecting your mind and what you think, because what you think will manifest itself in how you talk and how you behave. God cares about how we think.

Satan Cares how We Think!

Jesus said that Satan is a liar. The evil one occupies himself with distorting the truth—his main goal is to warp our thinking with skewed information. Jesus goes on to say about Satan, "there is no truth in him. When he lies, he speaks his native language, for he is a liar and the father of lies" (John 8:44).

Satan is also called the "devil." The Greek word for "devil" is *diabolos*, from which we get our English word "diabolical." A diabolical person is prone to fiendish ways—as for the devil, he is hell-bent on fiendish and deceptive ways of perverting truth. Truth has to do with ideas and propositional realities that we assimilate with our minds. Satan's full-time preoccupation is directed at attacking our minds—how we think about truth. Satan knows the all-important truth that behavior follows thinking. If Satan can get us to think the wrong way, then he will succeed in getting us to live the wrong way.

Here 2 Corinthians 4 is instructive. It plainly tells us Satan's *modus operandus* for keeping people from following God—he first attacks the mind of man. "The god of this age [Satan] has blinded the minds of unbelievers, so that they cannot see the light of the gospel of the glory of Christ" (verse 4). Satan is most successful when he can deceive people about truth, about how they think.

When Satan wanted to discredit Christ in the wilderness, he did not try to undermine Him primarily on a physical level. Rather, he attacked Christ's mind. He tried to distort biblical truth, by twisting the Scriptures, in order to get Jesus to disobey the Father and sin. Satan assaulted Christ's thought-life three times in a row. He wanted Jesus to think the wrong way (Matthew 4:1-11).

Revelation 12:9 says that currently Satan is attempting to "lead the whole world astray." He is doing this by evil "schemes" "in the heavenly realms" (Ephesians 6:11-12). This means that Satan is attacking humanity in the realm of ideas, ideologies, philosophies, worldviews, and religious beliefs. In other words, Satan is primarily concerned with what and how people think. He is the ultimate Minister of false propaganda.

The Main Battleground is the Mind

Because God puts a premium on what and how we think, and because the Devil's first line of attack is our thought-life, the main battleground in the Christian life is the mind.

According to Romans 12

Paul knew this basic truth. He commanded Christians to offer their "bodies as living sacrifices, holy and pleasing to God—this is your spiritual act of worship" (Romans 12:1). His expectation is that Christians live a life pleasing to God. But how do you do that, Paul? He gives the answer in the next verse. He goes on to say that in order to live right, one first must think right: "Do not conform any longer to the pattern of this world, but be transformed by the renewing of your mind. Then you will be able to test and approve what God's will is" (vs. 2). In other words, you live a godly life by controlling your mind.

Paul tells the Roman Christians there are two ways to help control the mind—one positive and one negative. And they must go together. First Paul speaks negatively. The word for "pattern" comes from the Greek word *schemata*, which refers to an external molding influence. And the verb "conform" is passive, which means it's an outward influence.

Paul is telling Christians to avoid getting squeezed into the wrong thinking mold. This wrong mold is the "world" or literally "this age." "This age" refers to the spirit of the age, the current ideas, beliefs, ideologies, philosophies and opinions in the unbelieving world that rule the day. So

Paul is warning Christians to refrain from being brainwashed by the world's false ideas, beliefs and convictions.

Current false beliefs in our day are numerous and include socialism, humanism, Darwinism, atheism, agnosticism, hedonism, sensualism, materialism, ecumenism, political correctness, pluralism, multiculturalism, feminism, relativism, subjectivism, deconstructionism, postmodernism, liberalism, pantheism, and Islam, to name a few. As Christians, we need to tenaciously protect our minds from these false ideologies that confront us at every turn.

Positively, Paul said we need to fill our minds with the right information. We do this by "transforming [our] minds." The word for "transform" in Romans 12:2 is *metamorphousthe*, from which we get "metamorphosis." "Metamorphosis" in the New Testament refers to an external change that is consistent with, or driven by, an inner reality.

For the Christian, this refers to the transformation in our behavior resulting from the indwelling Holy Spirit. The Spirit who lives in us since the moment of salvation is trying to change us on the inside into conformity with Christ (2 Corinthians 3:18). The Holy Spirit effects this change by working through our "mind." He wants to control our thoughts. For the Spirit knows that if He can control our thoughts, then He can control our lives.

The main way the Holy Spirit seeks to control our minds is through our intake of scriptural knowledge. The Spirit uses the supernatural truth of the Word to supernaturally change us from the inside out. So if you want to have godly living, you have to have godly thinking. And if you want to have godly thinking then you have to be taking in the truth of the Bible on a regular, daily basis. This is what Paul meant when he commanded Christians to, "Let the word of Christ dwell in you richly" (Colossians 3:16). Our minds need to be routinely saturated with biblical truth if we want to live right and think right in this godless age.

According to 2 Corinthians 10

Every Christian is a soldier (2 Timothy 2:3), and every believer is involved in a war—a war over the soul, and a war to the death. That's how serious the stakes are when it comes to religion. Our battle is not on a human or physical level, but rather on a supernatural and spiritual level. We are at war with sin (Romans 7:23), death (1 Corinthians 15:26), hell (Matthew 16:18), lies (1 Timothy 4:2), and the Devil himself (1 Peter 5:8). In 2 Corinthians 10 Paul tells the Christian how to successfully prepare for and wage such a spiritual battle:

> *For though we live in the world, we do not wage war as the world does. The weapons we fight with are not the weapons of the world. On the contrary, they have divine power to demolish strongholds. We demolish arguments and every pretension that sets itself up against the knowledge of God, and we take captive every thought to make it obedient to Christ (vv. 3-5).*

Paul was the most valiant Christian warrior that ever lived. He was executed as a martyr for his faith. But Paul was no Crusader. He carried no sword, rifle, armor, bullets, or grenade-launcher. That's because he did not engage in physical fights. This passage tells us what kind of battle Paul was embroiled in constantly. He gave himself full-time to the battle of the mind—he was a soldier for the truth. He gave his life to preserve spiritual revelation.

The key to understanding the context of this passage is to focus on what it is that Paul "demolished." He demolished "arguments," "pretensions," and false "knowledge." That means Paul was warring against human and demonic ideas, philosophies, religious teachings, opinions, theories and worldviews that were contrary to the truth of God. And Paul knew that this war was waged in the human mind. That's why he said the key to victory was to take every false notion, thought, or speculation prisoner and bring them into subjection to the truth of Christ. God's truth was his "weapon."

This is the key to true spiritual victory in life. We need to think right in order to live right. We need to put a premium on the preservation, propagation and application of biblical truth in our lives above all else. Contrast this idea of victorious spiritual living with other, more popular and prominent suggestions so frequently touted in the Christian community: mysticism, asceticism, exorcism, legalism, separatism, pietism, civil disobedience, political activism. Instead, we should keep vigilant guard against all information coming our way, vetting out all that is false.

"Peace of Mind" is All in the Mind

True peace of mind is a highly coveted and often elusive commodity here in America. This is made evident by virtue of the ever-increasing number of people taking anti-depressant medications to calm their nerves, eliminate fear, curb anxiety and stabilize their emotions. Countless others are pursuing tranquility through Eastern meditation, *mantras*, *yoga*, bio-feedback, the zodiac, Zen, the Kabbalah, psychiatry, acupuncture, and many other means.

An historical paradigm for peace of mind

According to the Bible, the Christian has a clear alternative in the pursuit of "peace of mind," which Paul explains in Philippians. He tells the believers at Philippi how to attain true "mind control":

> *Do not be anxious about anything, but in everything, by prayer and petition, with thanksgiving, present your requests to God. And the peace of God, which transcends all understanding, will guard your hearts and your minds in Christ Jesus (4:6-7).*

If you are a Christian and want true, supernatural peace of mind, freedom from panic attacks, victory over agoraphobia, and a clear strategy for combating anxiety and recurrent depression, then this passage is for you! Paul delineates several specific truths here with the goal of providing the Christian with "peace of mind."

One basic truth to recognize here is that Paul emphatically states that this is a promise from God. God always keeps His promises. And if a believer does what this verse commands, he will be assured the answer, which is "peace of mind." Actually it's better than peace of mind, for Paul specifically says it is the "peace of God" which will guard your "hearts and minds." The heart and mind refers to our emotions and thoughts. That is key, because "anxiety" is the lack of control over the thoughts and emotions. And it is the peace "of God," which is a supernatural, heavenly peace that is promised.

Another truth to consider is Paul's first command which has to do with "prayer." This specifically refers to talking to God. When you have anxiety, first talk to God, worship Him, focus on Him and His greatness—get your mind, your thoughts on Him. In other words, get your eyes, and mind, off yourself and your problems, and fix them on God's greatness. That is the first step to overcoming an anxious mind.

The next step, after focusing on God in prayer, is "petition." This word refers to praying for others; interceding on their behalf to God. It specifically refers to asking God to reach out in mercy to those who are struggling or are in need of God's grace in any given area. In other words, get your eyes and your mind off your own problems and think about other people's problems and pray for God to intervene. There will always be other people we know who have more or bigger problems and trials than we do. When we begin to look at our problems in light of other people's greater problems, it tends to change our perspective for the good. It positively affects our minds and emotions. Our problems suddenly don't seem so insurmountable.

The next step to overcoming troubled thoughts and emotions, after focusing on God and focusing on others, is to be filled with "thanksgiving." Here Paul says the Christian should always be giving thanks to God for all He has done. Every Christian has much to be thankful for: Jesus, salvation, forgiveness, the promise of heaven, the treasure of the Word, the indwelling Holy Spirit, and on and on. In other words, get your eyes and mind off your problems and fixate them on your blessings. This will change your perspective. This will affect your thought life for the better and in turn, your emotions will follow suit.

The last step to fighting off anxiety, after you have thought about God, others, and your blessings, is to "present your requests to God." In other words, after you have trained and disciplined your mind to focus on the proper priorities, you are then in a position to tell God about your problems. God is our Father and cares for us and our needs more than we care about our own children; hence the invitation to present all of our specific requests to Him. Peter reminds us about "casting all your anxiety on him because he cares for you" (1 Peter 5:7).

The key to overcoming anxiety, fear, worry, fretting, and emotional instability is to have the right priorities in our thought life; to be deliberate thinkers. And the secret is to be other-oriented, not self-centered; to fix our thoughts on God, others and our blessings—not our problems. That's the essence of mature Christian living.

Paul goes on even further about having peace of mind by exercising proper mind control. He writes,

> *Finally, brothers, whatever is true, whatever is noble, whatever is right, whatever is pure, whatever is lovely, whatever is*

*admirable—if anything is excellent or praiseworthy—**think** about such things....And the God of peace will be with you (Philippians 4:8-9).*

Once again Paul promises believers that they can have the "peace of God." And once again the key to attaining it is based on how we "think." The word for "think" in this passage is from *logizo* from which we get our English word "logic." It has to do with how we think, reason, and process intellectual information. And the verb here is in the present tense, which means this needs to be a continual, ongoing habit—a lifestyle of right thinking. Paul is commanding Christians here to routinely and deliberately think, ponder, ruminate and concentrate on good thoughts.

We think on things we are exposed to. Our mind is fed thoughts from the material we read, the movies we watch, the news we listen to, the music we hear, the conversations we have, the entertainment we engage in and more. The Christian needs to constantly ask, "Is this information I am exposed to 'true,' 'noble,' 'right,' 'pure,' 'lovely,' etc?" The Bible determines what is "true," "noble," "right," etc. In other words, all the information that enters our mind needs to be screened through the grid of the Bible. Once again, we are reminded that right living results from right thinking.

A modern day testimony of peace of mind

I will never forget the time when I had a Christian friend who battled with anxiety in all of its modern forms: panic attacks, depression, hyperactivity, ADD, emotional instability, etc. This person had a personal psychiatrist, a psychologist, and was taking an assortment of pills a day in an attempt to cope with the problem. This had gone on for years. It was not working. So my friend sought my advice.

I simply opened up Philippians 4 to him, read verses 6-9, and carefully explained, at length and in detail, the great promise God has given us here about true peace of mind. I gave my friend a homework assignment to practice the truths Paul delineates in the passage. I held him accountable on his daily prayer life as Paul outlined here. I exhorted him to get his eyes off himself and onto God, other's problems, and on his blessings. He agreed to try—he was at the end of his rope.

Over the course of months there was moderate improvement. I moved out of the area and we did not have contact for quite some time. Then about three years later, I got a letter from him telling the story of how God supernaturally was healing him from chronic anxiety. Gradually he was able to wean himself off the numerous drugs he was consuming daily and was becoming more disciplined in a vital prayer life. Today, almost five years later, he testifies to the true power of God's promise to give real peace of mind if we follow His ways as outlined in Scripture.

Examine Everything Carefully

Earlier I mentioned the dangerous beliefs and teachings in the non-Christian world that believers need to guard against. Amazingly, the Christian actually has to be even more wary of the dangerous teachings that are being promulgated inside the church. This can be difficult to imagine, but it's true. Paul and the other New Testament writers knew this truth. They warned the church repeatedly about pseudo-Christian teachings, masquerading in quasi-biblical jargon, infesting, deceiving and poisoning the church. Paul warned the pastors of Ephesus with these words:

> *Keep watch over yourselves and all the flock...I know that af-*
> *ter I leave, savage wolves will come in among you and will not*
> *spare the flock. Even from your own number men will arise*
> *and distort the truth...* (Acts 20:28-30).

Here Paul calls religious false teachers "savage wolves." And Paul makes it clear that many of these savages-to-come will arise "from your own number." That means that some false teachers will rise up from *inside* the church. They'll look like Christians, talk like Christians, and even do lip-service to the Bible as an authority. On the outside they "appear" to be Christian—but on the inside they are "savage wolves."

From reading Paul's thirteen epistles it is clear that he wrote to Christian churches to solve their problems. One of the biggest problems churches had was the proliferation of false teaching. And the majority of those false teachings came from false teachers who had either infiltrated the church or who had grown up in the church. Most of the damnable heresies Paul was contending with were fabricated from within the church.

Things have not changed a bit in 2,000 years; today's American church has the same problem. We have a rampant proliferation of false teaching in every quarter of the church. And the reason it is so dangerous is that it is so close to the truth. That's the danger of counterfeit money. The closer it looks to the original, the harder it is to identify and scrutinize. But we need to scrutinize. We need to carefully discern everything that is set forth as spiritual truth. Just because something is on so-called "Christian" television, does not mean it's good or biblical. Unfortunately, Christian book stores are littered with a myriad of books that simply are not Christian or biblical.

So the Christian needs to "think, think, think." This is one of the most important, yet most forgotten spiritual disciplines for the believer. Paul commanded all Christians to, "Test everything. Hold on to the good. Avoid every kind of evil" (1 Thessalonians 5:21-22). The word for "test" here means "examine, judge, scrutinize, prove." And Paul is speaking in reference to spiritual and religious teachings. The verb is in the present tense, which means this is to be an ongoing, continual habit for the Christian—a lifestyle of discerning thinking. Not everything coming down the pike is kosher or true.

The apostle John gave the church a similar warning: "Dear friends, do not believe every spirit, but test the spirits to see whether they are from God, because many false prophets have gone out into the world" (1 John 4:1). In other words, John is saying, "Christian, don't believe everything you hear, see or read...even if the teacher said he was a Christian...because he may have been tricking you."

That kind of trickery is going on in the church today. Below are some popular false religious heresies that are being passed off as "Christian," but in reality they are dressed-up, old, unbiblical teachings in modern array and manifestations. Beware of the following notions that are alive and festering well in today's church:

God is the Creator...but He needed a little help—for seventeen centuries the church taught what the Bible taught...that God created all things out of nothing in the beginning, just like Genesis 1-3 says. But since the rise of rationalism and skepticism that began in the 1700's, the veracity and historicity of the Creation account has been under siege in the church. Today, it is hard to find a Christian college, seminary, commentary or Bible teacher who takes Genesis literally. Many have caved in to the intimidation of modern secular science, which is simply human speculation (1 Timothy 6:20). With respect to origins, they aver: "Evolution is a fact." But God said emphatically, "in six days the LORD made the heavens and the earth" (Exodus 20:11). Jesus and Paul took the Creation account literally (Mark 10:5-9; Romans 5), so we can too.

God wants you rich!—the 1970's saw the rise of the "health, wealth, and prosperity gospel" on the fringes of popular Christianity—now it dominates the foreground, as evidenced by the proliferation of current best-selling books authored by the next wave of prosperity teachers and preachers. The truth is, God might not want you to be rich; actually, He might want you to be poor. Peter, the head apostle, told a beggar one day, "silver or gold I do not have" (Acts 3:6). Jesus did not have material wealth and He even warned against the pursuit of it (Matthew 6:19-24).

Having a lot of money and possessions is not a litmus test for spirituality. It's not how much you have; it's what you do with what you have. God will determine how much you need. The Bible says, "The LORD sends poverty and wealth" (1 Samuel 2:7). That's an amazing statement. When was the last time you heard a Christian say or teach that "God sends poverty"? That is a scandalously, politically incorrect thought. But God's Word says it's true. When you hear a so-called Bible teacher who is always talking about getting "money, money, money"— you can be assured that is a false teacher (Philippians 1:17; 2 Peter 2:1, 3; Jude 16).

God knows everything...almost—unbelievably there is a growing acceptance in today's church of what is called "Open Theism." It is the ridiculous and blasphemous notion that God does not know the future, for the future has not happened yet. But Peter said to Jesus, "Lord, you know all things" (John 21:17). God said in Isaiah, "I make known the end from the beginning, from ancient times, what is still to come" (46:10). In the original Hebrew this verse means, "God knows everything, even the future that has not happened yet." Case closed.

God helps those who help themselves—this is one of the oldest false, humanistic adages that gets circulated in Christian circles. The truth is just the opposite—we can't help ourselves...we are helpless. And God takes pleasure in helping the helpless. We can't save ourselves; we can't earn forgiveness (Ephesians 2:8-9). Every good gift is from God, and salvation is His greatest gift. But sinful man is inherently prideful, always wanting to earn approval through works-righteousness. Today we have the "New Perspective" growing in popularity in the church. It's the old heresy that says, "we are saved by grace plus human effort." It undermines and even denies the biblical   doctrine of salvation by faith alone through God's grace. Anytime you smell a teaching, and it reeks of works-righteousness to any degree, then you can be sure that it is not of God. Those who help themselves don't need God's help. Jesus said it was not the healthy who needed a physician, but the sick (Luke 5:31).

Men and women are equal...in all ways—men and women were created equal by God in terms of value, dignity and inherent worth (Genesis 1:26-27; Galatians 3:28). Unfortunately, secular feminism has crept into the church and has in effect over-turned God's ordained roles for men and women. The Bible does not teach that men and women are equal in all ways. For example, women have babies, men don't. Males are daddies, females are mommies. Men and women are to maintain distinctions with respect to functional roles as God has defined them.

Husbands are to be the heads in the home (1 Corinthians 11:3). Women are to respect the leadership of their husbands (1 Peter 3:1-6). God has ordained men to lead the local church by serving as the pastors, elders, overseers and proclaimers of doctrine (1 Timothy 2-3). Women have just as important ministry roles in the church in the areas of teaching, discipleship, counseling and service; but the areas in which they are to serve are to be consistent with their calling as women. The New Testament defines those parameters. Today, countless churches are ordaining women as pastors, bishops, elders and preachers in clear defiance of Scripture.

If it works, it must be true—pragmatism is ubiquitous in America's church. After all, getting the job done is the American way. "The ends justify the means," is the slogan of the day. More and more churches are displacing theology and foundational doctrines with the latest market-ing schemes and business principles. Savvy CEO's are preferred over biblically qualified "divines." Local churches are vying to replicate the latest method, fad, or secret model that will usher in success by increas-ing the numbers. But the Bible says that if it works, it might not be true. And if it's true, it might not even work—at least when results are assessed by human standards. Paul was chased out of nearly every city he pastored. Jesus said there would be "few" who would positively respond to the gospel (Matthew 7:14). Jesus never promised outward, human success in church work. Rather, Jesus promised His disciples that, "the world hates you" (John 15:19).

If it's new, it must be true–the "New Perspective" is trying to slither its way into mainstream Evangelical Christianity. It's the view that says we've had it all wrong about what the Apostle Paul had to say about justification. Some influential, heavy-hitting, highfalutin theological scholars are trying to tell the church that we need to re-examine what we have been taught for centuries about Paul's theology. They say that justification has nothing to do with salvation (or the doctrine of *soteriology*) and that salvation is not a forensic declaration (a one time, past completed action by God as Judge), but rather it's a process. They say God's righteousness is not imputed to the believer, even though 2 Corinthians 5:21 says it is. They say the Pharisees were actually good guys, who had a respectable religious faith, even though Jesus called them "hypocrites" (Matthew 23:13), "son[s] of hell" (Matthew 23:15), "blind guides" (Matthew 23:16), "fools" (Matthew 23:17), "full of greed" (Matthew 23:25), "whitewashed tombs" (Matthew 23:27), "snakes...vipers" (Matthew 23:33), murderers (Matthew 23:34), and offspring of Satan (John 8:44). The biggest red flag about the "New Perspective" view has to do with the original progenitors of this system of thinking—every one of them were men who denied the complete inerrancy and sufficiency of the Bible.

"God spoke to me!"–has a fellow Christian ever said that to you? When I hear that, I get queasy. God has declared that He speaks through His written Word, the Bible, in these last days (Hebrews 1:1-2). The Bible is sufficient (2 Timothy 3:16-17). God is not giving ongoing, supernatural, direct revelation to an elite few who happen to be more spiritual and more in touch with the Almighty than the rest of us (Jude 3; Revelation 22:18-19).

God's complete written revelation is available to all Christians. Although God is not speaking audibly today, He does prompt us through our conscience, the indwelling Holy Spirit and other Christians, but it is always in keeping with His revealed will as found in the Bible. To claim that Jesus is making special guest appearances to an elite few, or that God is speaking audibly to some apart from His Word, is to deny the sufficiency and authority of the Bible (1 Peter 1:8; 1 Corinthians 4:6).

It's all about unity—many people in the church put a premium on unity...at any cost. "Can't we all just get along?" is the hue and cry. It sounds spiritual, but it's naïve, unrealistic and unbiblical. Paul wrote thirteen letters to the early churches. Every one of those letters was written to deal with conflict and problems in the church (1 Corinthians 11:19). Conflict results from sin, and all Christians are sinners; so conflict in the church is inevitable and inescapable. True spiritual health is not gauged by whether there is division or not; it's gauged by how that division is managed biblically and in a Christ-like manner.

"What would Jesus Do?" Well, we do know that He was not good at making friends and influencing everyone. He had many enemies. He had enemies because people are sinners, and most sinners hate the truth. The Bible commands Christians to be unified around the truth (Ephesians 4:14-16). There is no real unity apart from the truth. Jesus said He was the truth (John 14:6), and that the Word was truth (John 17:17). Real Christian unity will orbit around the Person and work of Jesus Christ and the truth of His Word, the Bible. But in this day and age, those topics are taboo and politically incorrect. So much for unconditional unity.

It's all about relevance—some in the church today believe our priority is in trying to be relevant to the postmodern society in which we live. Therefore, they say we need to "deconstruct" all our old, traditional paradigms of doing church. We need to be hip, respectable, and make Christianity user-friendly and comfortable. We need to dim the lights, crank up the music, abandon Christian lingo, tone down the preaching, do more skits, confiscate the pews, re-arrange the chairs, jettison the tie, forget the hymnal, hide the Bible, beef up our marketing, and make Jesus appealing. But these are all superficial gimmicks that don't redeem the soul. Only the truth of the gospel will do that. The gospel, or the message about who Jesus is and what He did, "is the power of God for the salvation of everyone who believes" (Romans 1:16). But the fact of the matter is, many people just don't want to believe. Jesus said that some people love sin more than they love truth (John 3:19). Changing the furniture, the ambiance or your approach won't change their minds.

Questions for Review

1. What is the main distinctive of "postmodernism"?

_____

_____

_____

_____

2. How can the Christian know that truth is knowable?

_____

_____

_____

3. What is Paul's pattern of writing in his epistles relative to doctrine vs. practical living?

_____

_____

_____

_____

4. What does "doctrine" mean?

_____

_____

_____

_____

5. What did Jesus mean when He commanded us to "love God with all your mind"?

_____

_____

_____

6. According to 2 Corinthians 4, what is Satan's main plan of attack?

_____

_____

_____

7. According to Romans 12:1-2, what is the key to right living?

_____

_____

_____

8. According to 2 Corinthians 10, what are the "strongholds" that Paul was demolishing?

_____

_____

_____

9. Discuss how you can apply Philippians 4:8 to your life? What music do you listen to? Are the lyrics true, biblical and moral or worldly, sensual and false? What books do you read? Do the books you read prompt you to dwell on heavenly things or earthly things? What TV shows do you watch? Do they comply with or contradict biblical truth? What is your mind dwelling on?

_____

_____

_____

_____

_____

_____

_____

10. What obligation does each Christian have to guard against false teaching that is prevalent in the church?

_____

_____

_____

_____

For further study on *Think!* see these helpful resources:
The Coming Evangelical Crisis, edited by John Armstrong
Renewing Your Mind in a Mindless World, by James Boice
Inerrancy, by Norman Geisler
Loving God With All Your Mind, by Elizabeth George
Christianity in Crisis, by Hank Hanegraaff
The Agony of Deceit, by Michael Horton
The Seduction of Christianity, by Dave Hunt
Invasion of Other Gods, by David Jeremiah
Give Me an Answer, by Cliff Knechtle
Mind Siege, by Tim LaHaye
Think Biblically, by John MacArthur
Kingdom of the Cults, by Walter Martin
Every Thought Captive, by Richard Pratt, Jr.
How Should We Then Live, by Francis Schaeffer
Scripture Twisting, by James Sire
Decisions, Decisions, by Dave Swavely
Who Am I?, by Robert L. Thomas
The Roman Catholic Controversy, by James White

11

Obey!

"to obey is better than sacrifice"
(1 Samuel 15:22)

Obedience is synonymous with living a godly life. From the beginning of time God has required His people to obey Him. With the first human God ever created, God promised blessing for obedience and punishment for disobedience (Genesis 2:15-17). In the days of Moses God promised the nation of Israel corporate blessing if they obeyed Him:

> *If you fully obey the LORD your God and carefully follow all his commands I give you today, the LORD your God will set you high above all the nations on earth. All these blessings will come upon you and accompany you if you obey the LORD your God (Deuteronomy 28:1-2).*

At the end of his life, Solomon wisely concluded that there is really just one main, paramount objective for humanity in this life, and that is to obey God. That is the real purpose of this life. He said, "Fear God and keep his commandments, for this is the whole duty of man. For God will bring every deed into judgment, including every hidden thing, whether it is good or evil" (Ecclesiastes 12:13-14). This is from a man who had it all—wealth, fame, power, privilege, and women. And none of it truly fulfilled him.

Jesus Himself taught that the essence of being a believer was living a life of obedience to Him:

> *If anyone would come after me, he must deny himself and take up his cross daily and follow me. For whoever wants to save his life will lose it, but whoever loses his life for me will save it (Luke 9:23-24).*

In the last chapter of the Bible, Jesus warns humanity that in the future every soul that ever lived will be judged based on their obedience or disobedience in light of God's commands (Revelation 22:12-17). From beginning to end, the Bible mandates obedience from all people to God the Creator. In light of that sobering truth, let's survey some basic biblical principles on obedience that Christians should prioritize in their daily living.

What is "Obedience"?

The word used most frequently in the Bible to denote "obey" or "obedience" is the word "hear." The Old Testament word for "hear" is *shema*. This is the word used in the most famous verse memorized by Jews—Deuteronomy 6:4—the *Great Shema*, which states, "**Hear, O Israel: The LORD our God, the LORD is one.**" In the New Testament, the common word for "hear" is *akouo* from which we get our English word acoustics, and related words that have to do with auditory reception—the things we "hear" with our ears. The Bible takes this notion of hearing and applies it to obedience to emphasize the importance of listening to God's voice through His Word. To truly listen to God is to obey Him. This is what Jesus meant when He said, "My sheep listen to [hear] My voice...and they follow Me" (John 10:27).

Frequently in the New Testament, the preposition *hupo* (which means "under") is added to the front of the word *akouo* to add emphasis to the notion of obeying God. It can literally be translated as "to hear under" or "to listen under" (*to look up to*) and means to get in line under the authority of someone else and comply with his commands. It is at times synonymous with "submit to." An example of this compound use of "to hear under" is in Ephesians 6:1, where God commands children to "**obey** your parents in the Lord, for this is right." So the idea of submission is at the heart of biblical obedience.

To obey is more than just hearing what God commands—it's hearing and doing what God commands. True obedience includes right actions. This is what Jesus meant when he said the wise man "hears these words of mine, and puts them into practice" (Matthew 7:24). Lip service without compliant follow-through is disobedience.

True obedience also includes right attitudes. It means doing what God says to do, not with just the right actions, but also with the right heart. I can tell my son to take out the trash. He can follow through with the right actions, while at the same time be mumbling, grumbling and complaining the whole time under his breath with a bad attitude because he does not feel like taking out the trash. That is not biblical obedience. Going through the motions with the wrong heart and an unsubmissive spirit is disobedience. Ephesians 6:1 says children should "obey" their parents. That means they should have the right actions. But Ephesians 6:2 goes on to command children to "honor" their parents. That means they should obey their parents with the right attitude. The Bible refers to this as obeying "from the heart" (Romans 6:17). So true biblical obedience means doing what God says with the right actions and the right attitudes. The two must go together.

Why do Christians Obey?
Not to earn forgiveness

The Bible assumes that Christians will be people who are characterized by obedience to God's commands. Peter refers to Christians as those who "obey the truth" (1 Peter 1:22). Paul calls Christians "slaves to...obedience" (Romans 6:16). John says that obedience to God is the fruit of salvation and the mark of a true believer (1 John 2:3-6). The Bible calls Christians "followers," a graphic metaphor picturing a lifestyle of obedience and submission to God (1 Corinthians 11:1; Ephesians 5:1, KJV). In contrast, unbelievers are called "the children of disobedience" (Ephesians 2:2; 5:6, KJV). Their lives are characterized by sinful living and disobedience to God's commands either in action, attitude or both.

But why do Christians obey? Or, why should they and why would they have the desire to do so? Most people in the world are religious or spiritual. And most people would say they try to obey their god religiously. But what motivates non-Christians to obey God is vastly different from what motivates Christians to obey God.

The Bible teaches that Christians obey God because He bestowed favor on them in Christ by His unmerited grace. Non-Christians who are religious try to obey God to earn His favor, to win His acceptance and approval, or to work for forgiveness and salvation. This is the key distinction between biblical Christianity and virtually every false religion on earth. The Bible says we are to obey God because we are forgiven, not to earn forgiveness. False religion teaches salvation by works—the idea that you can earn God's approval and forgiveness by doing as many good deeds as possible.

But the Bible categorically rejects and condemns the notion that sinful humans can earn God's forgiveness by good works. Ephesians 2:8-9 clearly says, "For it is by grace you have been saved, through faith—and this not from yourselves, it is the gift of God—not by works, so that no one can boast." Salvation is a gift. You can't earn it. You can't work for it. Trying to obey and follow the Ten Commandments to the best of your ability will not make you a Christian, will not earn God's approval, will not get you into heaven, and will not forgive any of your sins. Unfortunately, this is precisely what many mistakenly think Christianity and the Bible teach. But it's the very antithesis of what the Bible teaches about salvation (Titus 3:4-8).

According to the Bible, only Jesus' obedience earned God's forgiveness for sinners (Romans 5:18-19). If you want God's approval, acceptance, forgiveness and the assurance that you will go to heaven when you die, then there is only one way to do that (Acts 4:12). And that is to put your faith in Jesus' obedience, for He lived a sinless life, willingly died on the cross as the punishment for all sin. Then He rose bodily from the grave, proving His authority over sin, death and the Devil. This is what the Bible calls the good news, or the gospel. Believing in the gospel of Jesus Christ is all a person can do to be saved (Mark 1:14-15; John 6:28-29; Romans 1:16; 1 Corinthians 15:1-5).

Because of the indwelling Holy Spirit

It is plain that Christians don't try to obey God to get forgiven...they obey God because they are forgiven. Believers should want to obey God as an act of devotion, love and thanksgiving in light of the fact that He graciously saved them from sin. John the Apostle put it this way: "This is love: not that we loved God, but that he loved us and sent his Son as an atoning sacrifice for our sins....We love because he first loved us" (1 John 4:10, 19).

The moment a person puts faith in Jesus Christ and His gospel, that person is saved by God and He instantly sends His Holy Spirit to live inside the new believer permanently (1 John 3:24). The Holy Spirit imparts a new mind and worldview into the believer (1 Corinthians 2:16). The Christian also gains for the first time real supernatural spiritual capacities, like the desire to obey and love God from the heart (Romans 5:5). The Holy Spirit even gives the Christian the actual ability to obey God, not just the desire to do so (1 Peter 1:2).

Over the years I have heard Christians, even pastors and Bible teachers, say, "Well, none of us can do anything for God with pure motives." I'd say, "Yes we can." And the reason I say that is because the indwelling Holy Spirit makes it possible for a believer to obey God with pure motives. Paul commended the Christians in Rome because they "obeyed [God] from the heart" (Romans 6:17). That means they had pure motives when they obeyed. Paul is not suspicious of their faith.

I remember a church elder one time who tried to convince me that we are all totally depraved. That is, he was arguing that the Bible teaches that Christians are totally depraved, and therefore they cannot obey God with pure motives...ever. But that is wrong. The Bible teaches that unbelievers—non-Christians—are totally depraved, lost in sin, offspring of the world and the Devil (Ephesians 2:1-3). But Christians are not totally depraved. Christians are totally forgiven, regenerated, adopted into the family of God and are made holy—totally pure in Christ before God (Ephesians 1:7; 2:4-6, 19). The New Testament calls Christians "saints" which literally means "holy ones." One of the main reasons Christians can be called "holy ones" is that the Holy Spirit now literally resides in them.

By virtue of the transforming work of salvation through Jesus Christ's death and resurrection and the indwelling Holy Spirit, Christians can obey God with the right actions and even the right motives.

Clearing up Misconceptions

One passage that frequently confuses people, even Christians, on the issue of how obedience relates to salvation is Philippians 2:12-13 which says,

Therefore, my dear friends, as you have always obeyed—not only in my presence, but now much more in my absence—continue to work out your salvation with fear and trembling, for it is God who works in you to will and to act according to his good purpose.

It is not uncommon to hear those who are confused about biblical salvation refer to a portion of this passage, quoting it out of context to make the case that we need to work real hard, and keep on working to earn and assure our salvation. They try to back it up by saying, "You know, the Bible says, 'work out your salvation with fear and trembling'." They turn this passage on its ear, trying to make it say what it actually does not teach. Nowhere does the Bible say we can work to earn, sustain, or secure our salvation. The very notion is devilish and undermines the sufficiency of Christ's atoning work on the cross and should be soundly rejected by Christians (Galatians 1:8-9).

The key to properly understanding this passage, and the verse quoted above, is to interpret it in light of the whole context. Bible verses and phrases have meaning only when read in their immediate contexts. This passage does say that Christians need to work out their salvation. But Paul does not mean that Christians need to try to earn their salvation or work so they can get saved. Christians have already been saved and possess salvation as an eternal gift. Here Paul is simply commanding Christians to grow with respect to the salvation they already have. He's telling them to keep growing as Christians. This is called "sanctification"—the process by which a believer matures in the Christian faith during the course of this life with the help of the indwelling Holy Spirit.

After Paul commands Christians to work out, or "live out," their salvation, he reminds them that it is only possible because of the indwelling Holy Spirit. He says, "it is God who works in you" (2:13). Here, he is referring to the indwelling Holy Spirit who took up residence in the believer at the moment of conversion when that person trusted in Christ. The Holy Spirit of God enables Christians to "work out" their salvation, or to grow and mature in the Christian life. This is similar to the promise Paul made to Christians at the beginning of this epistle when he guaranteed them that "he [God] who began a good work [initial salvation, or "justification"] in you [those who are already saved] will carry it on to completion until the day of Christ Jesus" (Philippians 1:6).

Philippians 2:12-13, then, is a command for Christians to grow spiritually, by living a life of obedience, in the power of the Holy Spirit of God, who comes to believers at the time of salvation. So Christians are expected to obey and are told they can obey by virtue of God's supernatural enabling.

What do We Obey?

Paul said his greatest goal was to always try to obey God. He writes,

> *So we make it our goal to please him [by obeying], whether we are at home in the body or away from it. For we must all appear before the judgment seat of Christ, that each one may receive what is due him for the things done while in the body, whether good or bad (2 Corinthians 5:9-10).*

All Christians should have the same desire—to please God in all they do. But how do we know what God wants? How does God communicate to humans? How do we figure out what God's will is on any given issue? How does God command us today? How do we hear His voice in the twenty-first century? Is He talking to anyone audibly or in visions and dreams or through living prophets today as He has done in the past? These are all important and relevant questions.

Those in the Mormon Church say they hear from God through their living Prophet, who is also called their President and Apostle. He supposedly gives divine revelation from God and speaks authoritatively for the Mormon Church. So Mormons are obligated to obey him. In addition, they have three books they call divine Scripture that they seek to obey: the *Book of Mormon*, the *Pearl of Great Price* and *Doctrine and Covenants*.

Hindus seek to obey the *Vedas* (holy writings) and a multitude of living spiritual leaders called gurus, who are actually believed to be incarnate deity. Muslims seek to obey various muftis, Imams, and *fatwas* all claiming to speak authoritatively on behalf of Allah, the God of Islam.

The Jehovah's Witnesses seek to obey the Governing Body of the Watchtower Bible and Tract Society. This Body is an autocratic form of rule by an elite group of people who dictate what God has and has not said.

People in the Roman Catholic Church look to the Pope, the Magisterium, Roman Catholic tradition and the institution of the Church as voices of authority whom they must obey.

Historic, biblical Christianity differs from all the above mentioned religions when it comes to the final source of authority. Biblical Christianity teaches that the sole authority on matters of religious faith and practice is the Bible. The Bible is the holy, inerrant, complete, sufficient, living Word of God. When the Bible speaks, God speaks. The sixty-six books of the Bible contain everything God wants the Church and each individual Christian to know. To obey the Bible is to obey God (Matthew 15:4). To obey God is to obey the Bible.

Jesus taught that the thirty-nine books of the Old Testament were the very words of God, and were therefore authoritative, binding, and infallible (Matthew 4:4; 5:17-18; Luke 24:25-27, 44-47; John 10:35). He said the same would be true about the New Testament that was to be composed by His select Apostles (John 14:26; 16:13; Galatians 1:11-12; 1 Thessalonians 2:13; 2 Timothy 3:16). They wrote down the words of Jesus, who Himself was God (2 Peter 1:20-21; 1 John 4:6; Revelation 1:1-2).

The Bible has authority over all church leaders, over the church, over tradition, over every individual Christian. The Bible is the authority of God Himself (John 17:17; Revelation 22:18-19). When we seek to obey God, that means we seek to obey His Word, the Bible.

Obeying is Hard Sometimes

Living the Christian life is difficult. Being holy is hard work. As a matter of fact, no one alive will obey God perfectly all the time. The only person on earth who ever did that was Jesus. He never sinned in His thirty-three years on earth (John 8:46; 2 Corinthians 5:21; Hebrews 4:15).

We, on the other hand, sin—even though we are Christians. The Bible is clear about that. 1 Kings 8:46 says, "there is no one who does not sin." Paul declared that "all [humans] have sinned" (Romans 3:23). James, the half brother of Jesus, said to a group of Christians, "We all stumble [sin] in many ways" (James 3:2). Notice how he includes himself in the indictment. John, the beloved Apostle, said, "If we claim to be without sin, we deceive ourselves and the truth is not in us" (1 John 1:8).

When you became a Christian, all your sins were totally forgiven because the punishment for all your sins fell on Jesus when He died on the cross (Colossians 2:13-14). He endured the consequences for all your iniquity, legally speaking (Isaiah 53:4-6). He was punished by God the Father for the sins of the world. But practically speaking, your sin nature was not eradicated or removed when you became a Christian. Your soul was redeemed and made alive, but your flesh remains, and will remain until you die or until Jesus returns and transforms you at the resurrection (Romans 8:22-24; Philippians 3:20-21). So in the meantime, all Christians have the residue of fallenness which the Bible calls "the flesh." The flesh is our remaining unredeemed humanity.

This means that every Christian has to contend with sin and temptation every day of life. Every believer is practically susceptible to just about any conceivable sin. The reason this is so is because Christians have the intruder of "sin" still living in them—an unwelcome trespasser, but resident nonetheless. Carefully read how Paul diagnosed the reality of indwelling sin in his own soul, even though he was a Christian and an Apostle of Christ:

> *[14]I am unspiritual, sold as a slave to sin. [15]I do not understand what I do. For what I want to do I do not do, but what I hate I do. [16]And if I do what I do not want to do, I agree that the law is good. [17]As it is, it is no longer I myself who do it, but it is <u>sin living in me</u>. [18]I know that <u>nothing good lives in me</u>, that is, in my sinful nature. For I have the desire to do what is good, but I cannot carry it out. [19]For what I do is not the good I want to do; no, the evil I do not want to do—this I keep on doing. [20]Now if I do what I do not want to do, it is no longer I who do it, but it is <u>sin living in me</u> that does it.*
>
> *[21]So I find this law at work: When I want to do good, <u>evil is right there</u> with me. [22]For in my inner being I delight in God's law; [23]but I see another law at work in the members of my body, waging war against the law of my mind and making me a prisoner of the law of sin at work within my members. [24]What a wretched man I am! Who will rescue me from this body of death? [25]Thanks be to God—through Jesus Christ our Lord!*
>
> *So then, I myself in my mind am a slave to God's law, but in the sinful nature a slave to the law of sin (Romans 7:14-25).*

The above passage is one of the most enlightening theological realities we should know. Paul makes some incredible assertions here about the reality of sin in the believer. He says "sin lives" in him as a Christian. He says "evil" lives in him. He says "nothing good" lives in him. That's all true with reference to his unredeemed humanity—that part of him that will be transformed when he meets Christ. But until that time, it thrusts him into a spiritual war within the soul. This reality is true of every Christian today as well, however spiritual one might seem.

Every Christian also has the Holy Spirit of God living within—the welcomed Holy Guest, who enables the believer to live a holy life. The Holy Spirit is at odds with our indwelling sin and vice versa. As a result, there is a daily civil war brewing in the heart, soul and mind of every Christian—the Holy Spirit versus the sinful flesh.

Paul describes this spiritual battlefront of the Christian's soul in Galatians:

> So I say, live by the Spirit, and you will not gratify the desires of the sinful nature. For the sinful nature desires what is contrary to the Spirit, and the Spirit what is contrary to the sinful nature. They are in conflict with each other, so that you do not do what you want. But if you are led by the Spirit, you are not under law (5:16-18).

It is important to remember that Paul is talking to Christians in this passage. He reminds them that they have indwelling sin, that they may manifest sinful desires, and that there is a real spiritual war going on in the soul. Paul was not naïve or ignorant about the ongoing enemy of indwelling sin. Sin was no longer the master of the believer, but it was a persistent, real and dangerous menace to the soul.

At the height of his ministry, Paul admitted that he was a sinner— "the worst" sinner of all, as a matter of fact (1 Timothy 1:15). He never claimed to be perfect or without sin (Philippians 3:12-14). Yet he did believe that all of his sins were forgiven: past, present and future. He considered himself perfect "in Christ."

This seems like a blatant contradiction, but it's not. It is a mystery, but not a contradiction. One just needs to understand two different realities. On the one hand, people in and of themselves are inherently evil. On the other hand, if someone has a personal relationship with Christ, then that person has a perfect legal standing before God the Judge based on the perfection of Christ. At some point in the future, when we meet Christ, Christians' indwelling sin will be eradicated and only then will we be   perfect in our practice and position. Until then, while we are in our fallen state, we will have to live with the antinomy of this dual reality that we are sinners, while at the same time we are considered by God to be sinless "in Christ."

The author of Hebrews best summarized the essence of this mystery when he wrote, "by one sacrifice [Jesus' death on the cross] he has made perfect forever [totally forgiven, a past completed action at the cross] those [Christians] who are being made holy [in this life, through the process of sanctification]" (10:14). So practically speaking, every Christian has to battle with the reality of indwelling sin, while at the same time the Christian is positionally or legally perfect before God based on the atoning death of Jesus Christ.

Strategies for Obedience

The reality of indwelling sin (and the truth that the believer will never be perfect in this life) can be discouraging for the Christian. Some get so discouraged by this thought that they develop a defeatist and pessimistic attitude. They say, "Well, I'm just going to keep on sinning anyway—no one is perfect. Sin is here to stay. Everyone has a vice—let me have mine. Why make such a big deal of trying to obey all the time?" Paul condemns that kind of carnal, short-sighted thinking (Romans 6:15-16).

Instead, the New Testament expects and even requires the Christian to live victoriously over sin. The Bible expects believers to live a life ordered by obedience. For example, the Apostle Peter matter-of-factly exhorts Christians to live such a life when he writes, "As obedient children, do not conform to the evil desires you had when you lived in ignorance. But just as he who called you is holy, so be holy in all you do; for it is written: 'Be holy, because I am holy' " (1 Peter 1:14-16). Peter does not allow for disobedience in the life of the Christian because of the reality of indwelling sin. There are no legitimate excuses for compromise. Christians are commanded to obey God.

In your ongoing battle with sin, consider the following biblical principles to aid you in the war toward victory and obedience:

Don't make excuses

God hates sin (Psalm 5:4-5). We need to hate it too. Don't get into the habit of accepting your sinful behavior. Satan wants you to think like that—to not take sin seriously. God takes it seriously, so must we. Think of some sins in your life. Then consciously determine to "hate" them. Ask God to help you despise sin. Proverbs 8:13 tells us "to hate evil." Becoming an obedient person starts with an attitude of loving God by hating sin (Psalm 97:10).

It will take time...a lifetime, as a matter of fact

Christians need to be realistic about becoming holy. God wants us to mature and become like Christ. But it won't happen overnight. Christian maturity takes time—it's progressive and incremental and happens little by little over the course of the whole Christian life. We'll never be perfect in this life, but God promises to help the Christian grow progressively through the help of the indwelling Holy Spirit. This is good news—God promises to help Christians spiritually mature. Paul said, "we [believers]...are being   transformed into his [Jesus'] likeness with ever-increasing glory, which comes from the Lord, who is the Spirit" (2 Corinthians 3:18). This verse should encourage Christians to be optimistic (for we will grow) and patient (for it happens over a period of time) about becoming obedient.

Don't isolate yourself

Much sin and compromise is committed in secret (Ephesians 5:12). Examine your own sin. Is it routinely done when you are isolated and by yourself? If so, then take heed and be preventative by purposing to not be isolated or by yourself for long periods of time. The Bible says that it is not good for a man to be alone (Genesis 2:18). A fool isolates himself. Don't trust yourself. "The spirit is willing but the flesh is weak" (Matthew 26:41, NASB). Whenever possible, be in the company of other believers.

Become accountable

The Bible says, "confess your sins to each other" (James 5:16). The Bible also says, "As iron sharpens iron, so one man sharpens another" (Proverbs 27:17). Becoming vulnerable to other people by way of confessing sin and admitting areas of weakness can help the Christian live a more obedient life. God empowers believers when they become accountable to each other for their actions. Is there someone in your life who holds you accountable on a regular basis for being obedient to God in all areas of life?

Recognize patterns of wrong behavior

Sometimes, when people become Christians later in life as adults, they find that they have developed patterns of sinful behavior that are hard to shake even after they have been saved. Whether it's anger, lust, sexual temptation, lying, speaking profanity, complaining, sarcasm, discontentment, laziness, stubbornness, excessive anxiety, or whatever, life-long patterns of behavior pose a severe trial for many believers.

Do you have any deeply rooted patterns of sinful behavior that are a carry-over from many years of ungodly living? If so, the place to begin to uproot it is to first admit it and confess it as sin to God. The first step to overcoming the problem is to acknowledge that the problem exists. Proverbs says, "He who conceals his sins does not prosper, but whoever confesses and renounces them finds mercy" (28:13).

Put off sinful patterns of behavior

After exposing sinful patterns of behavior, determine then to forsake such a lifestyle. It has to be a conscious choice. Paul calls this "putting off." Put off old behaviors and then replace them with new godly habits—put off and then put on. Paul says to "put off all these [evil] things...[and] put on" godly behaviors (Colossians 3:8, 12, KJV).

Replacing old, bad habits will take time—and it's hard to do. But with the help of the Holy Spirit, deliberate planning, focused prayer and accountability from Christian friends, real change is possible.

Practice the spiritual disciplines

This whole book has been about the spiritual disciplines of the Christian life. I have tried to distill down the fundamental priorities for

Christian living according to the Bible. We have to master the basics to establish a solid spiritual foundation. Those basics are the imperatives mentioned in this book. To live an obedient Christian life means to live a life that is characterized by true worship, Christian fellowship, joining a local church, serving regularly in your church, discipling other Christians, giving to the church, going into the world to share the gospel, studying God's Word daily, praying privately every day, and protecting your mind with the truth. If these habits become routine practices in your life, then you will have greater success in obeying God. And when you live a life of obedience, God will bless you for it.

In closing, consider the great rewards promised by the Psalmist to any believer who chooses to obey God with his or her life:

> *Blessed is the man who does not walk in the counsel of the wicked or stand in the way of sinners or sit in the seat of mockers. But his delight is in the law of the LORD, and on his law he meditates day and night. He is like a tree planted by streams of water, which yields its fruit in season and whose leaf does not wither.* <u>*Whatever he does prospers*</u> *(Psalm 1:1-3).*

Questions for Review

1. Write a biblical definition of "obey":

_____

_____

_____

2. What is the Greek word for "obey" in Ephesians 6:1 and what is its significance?

_____

_____

_____

3. Is obedience an option for Christians? Why or why not?

_____

_____

_____

_____

4. Some people believe that new believers can't be expected to obey like other believers; respond to that notion:

_____

_____

_____

5. Does Philippians 2:12-13 teach that we need to work to earn or even maintain our salvation? Explain:

_____

_____

_____

6. What is the Christian's ultimate spiritual authority? Give a verse to support your answer:

_____

_____

_____

7. What role does the Holy Spirit play in helping Christians obey?

_____

_____

_____

8. Explain the significance of Romans 7:14-25 and indwelling sin in the life of a believer:

_____

_____

_____

9. As you examine your life, are there any areas of sin that seem to be a habit or pattern of behavior that need to change? If so, what are they and how did they become a pattern or habit?

_____

_____

_____

_____

10. What strategies can you employ to help overcome such sinful habits? Who will hold you accountable?

_____

_____

_____

_____

For further study on *Obey!* **see these helpful resources:**
How to Help People Change, by Jay Adams
The Pursuit of Holiness, by Jerry Bridges
The Practice of Godliness, by Jerry Bridges
What Matters Most, by Tony Evans
Miracle of Life Change, by Chip Ingram
Slaying the Giants in Your Life, by David Jeremiah
Delighting God: How to Live at the Center of God's Will, by D. James
    Kennedy
The Enemy Within, by Kris Lundgaard
How to Meet the Enemy, by John MacArthur
Trust and Obey: Obedience and the Christian, by R. C. Sproul, et al.
Following Christ, by Joseph Stowell

Scripture Index

"Every Christian should desire to meet the living God face to face as expressed in the Bible. *Christian Living Beyond Belief* can serve as a roadmap to attaining that reality. The church of today needs to be teaching the truth with authority. And that is what Dr. McManis does in this must-read book."
Dr. Wayne Anderson, Director, *The King of Kings Foundation*, Los Altos, CA

"*Christian Living Beyond Belief* is absolutely refreshing! The adherence to Scripture as the source of teaching, results in a powerful biblical view of the function of the Body of Christ. The Church needs this closeness to the Word as it defines and fulfills its God-intended purpose in this generation. Read it and live a life that's 'beyond belief'."
Tom Chance, AWANA *Missionary*, North Central, CA

"This book sets forth in a clear, edifying manner the biblical basics of true church growth. A church must grow down and deep in its individuals before it will experience genuine God-given growth far and wide. McManis has given us a clear, easy to read, biblically based treatment of the basics for Christian growth. May the Lord use it for His glory and the good of His Church."
Steve Fernandez, President, *Cornerstone Seminary*, Vallejo, CA

"Any believer will greatly benefit from this book on the basic disciplines of the Christian life."
Dr. Norman Geisler, Dean, *Southern Evangelical Seminary*, Matthews, NC

"Cliff McManis is a man with a voice we can trust to 'rightly divide the Word of truth.' He is a former student, a friend, and a man of God whose life is devoted to communicating God's truth with accuracy."
Jim George, noted author and speaker

"A simple text about the basics in our Christian walk is rare to find. This text is such a book. It plainly describes and challenges the genuine follower of Christ to refocus one's life on the simple but crucial elements of a 'working' faith. I urge any who take their Christian walk seriously at all, to read this text carefully and implement it fully."
Tom Givens, Senior Pastor, *Grace Baptist Church*, Santa Clarita, CA

"Today, the emphasis is on numerical growth, gathering people into the church, and the depth of biblical teaching on the whole counsel of God has woefully declined. If people are going to be able to defend their faith, and especially, handle adversity in their lives, they will need to know and understand Scripture. This book by Dr. Cliff McManis seeks to accomplish that by 'distilling all the basics of Christian living down into simple, easy to understand priorities and principles'. May you be able to live a more godly life as you implement these principles."
Dr. Thomas Halstead, Chairperson, Department of Biblical Studies, *The Master's College*, Santa Clarita, CA

"Cliff McManis has provided a book that every Christian could use. One that is deliberately developed from what the Bible teaches on a multitude of subjects essential for healthy Christian growth. Instead of following the contemporary trend of attempting to blend

postmodern mysticism with the Bible, McManis presents a strictly biblical approach to the items he presents. If you want a biblical book that teaches biblical spirituality then *Christian Living Beyond Belief* is for you."
Dr. Thomas Ice, Noted author, conference speaker and theologian, Arlington, TX

"In contrast to the claims of the church growth movement, Cliff McManis demonstrates that real corporate growth must be measured in terms of individual spiritual growth. Cliff's approach is straightforward and biblical, and serves as a helpful resource for churches that want to grow the right way—with depth not just breadth."
John MacArthur, Pastor-Teacher, *Grace Community Church*, Sun Valley, CA

"How should we understand the question of church growth? Cliff McManis understands that the first focus should be on growing Christians. In *Christian Living Beyond Belief*, Pastor McManis offers keen and credible biblical teaching on the character of true spiritual growth and Christian discipleship. This book is filled with biblical insight and will help Christians to understand how they can glorify God and experience his blessings in their own lives and in their churches."
R. Albert Mohler, Jr., President, The Southern Baptist Theological Seminary, Louisville, KY

"With great clarity and conciseness, Cliff McManis lays out the foundational disciplines of the Christian life. New believers and seasoned Christians alike will find *Christian Living Beyond Belief* a valuable resource for living a life devoted to God."
Luis Palau, World-renowned evangelist, broadcaster, and author of *High Definition Life*

"This book is a refreshing and challenging look at Scripture and its application to everyday responsibilities that will enable every Christian to grow in their personal and corporate worship experience. I especially appreciate its thought-provoking questions at the end of every chapter to help ensure practical application."
Harold Stenfort, *Child Evangelism Fellowship (CEF) International*, Vice-Chairman, Los Altos, CA

"Every church is called to keep score and to play to win. How do we measure our progress? In this book you are holding, Dr. McManis offers a fresh and biblical perspective to the growth we all seek for ourselves and for our churches."
Bob Thomas, Jr., Senior Teaching Pastor, *Calvary Church Los Gatos*, CA

"Christian Living Beyond Belief is a refreshing reminder for some and perhaps a startling eye-opener for others about teachings in the Bible that deal with a Christian's responsibilities to his/her local church. Cliff McManis has provided a stimulating picture of how believers can pitch in to enrich their own Christian community and thereby enrich the secular community around them as well."
Dr. Robert L. Thomas, Professor of New Testament, *The Master's Seminary*, Sun Valley, CA

"Pastor McManis has done exactly what he set out to do—he has given us ALL, wherever we are in our Christian pilgrimage—a simple, readable and practical explanation of the spiritual disciplines. It is a clarion call to honor God in our daily lives by pursuing biblical priorities. I highly recommend it!"
Kay Tokar, Area Advisor (*retired*), *Bible Study Fellowship (BSF)*, Central California